I0517669

IN HIS IMAGE

Life Affirmations from The Bible: Discovering
God's Best for Mankind

Sinikka Pember-Coulter

Copyright Notice

Copyright © 2025, Sinikka Pember-Coulter.

All rights reserved. No part of this publication may be copied, reproduced, republished, translated, stored, or transmitted in any form or by any means— whether electronic, mechanical, digital, or otherwise - without the prior written permission of the publisher.

This book is the result of dedication, creativity, and countless hours of effort. Any resemblance to real persons, living or dead, is purely coincidental—or perhaps just the universe having a bit of fun.

Published by Kinetic Digital Publishers

www.kineticdigitalpublishers.com

For permissions, inquiries, or other correspondence, please visit our website.

ISBN eBook: 978-1-967623-48-8
ISBN Paperback: 978-1-967623-49-5
ISBN Hardcover: 978-1-967623-50-1
Library of Congress Number: 2025917191

Table of Contents

"Your word is a lamp to my feet and a light to my path,"

Psalm 119: 105 NKJV.

"I will turn the darkness into light before them,"

Isaiah 42:16 NIV.

"But you are a chosen race, a royal priesthood, a holy nation, a people belonging to God, that you may proclaim the praises of Him who called you out of darkness into His wonderful light."

I Peter 2: 9 NIV.

"For God, who said, 'Let there be light in the darkness,' has made this light shine in our hearts so we could know the glory of God that is seen in the face of Jesus Christ."

2 Corinthians 4:6 NLT.

SINIKKA PEMBER-COULTER

Foreword

We live in an era of uncertainty, where long-held truths are increasingly dismissed as myth. God, once regarded as the ultimate authority, is now often reduced to a mere figure of speech an outdated concept, reshaped to fit individual preferences. The moral and ethical standards once rooted in biblical teachings are seen as relics of the past, replaced by a culture that prioritizes self-determination and fleeting pleasure. In what we call an "age of enlightenment", we have, in many ways, distanced ourselves from the very foundation that once guided us.

But are there other options available? Is it possible to still believe in a God who created the world, and not only the world we know, but the entire universe we can barely grasp at? And that *in seven days*, as measured by the rotation of a tiny planet surrounded by seven other planets circling around a fire ball of energy in an obscure celestial neighborhood called the Milky Way? No way! Many would find this assertion absurd. That sounds impossible!

However, those who say so fail to realize that their very breath is also an impossibility when considering all the circumstances that have brought them to this moment from conception in their mother's womb, or, as sometimes happens these days, in a test tube. The odds against us are great indeed, and life on this planet of ours is not a walk in the park. We face physical, emotional, relational, financial, and spiritual challenges almost from the moment we are born. Life is not easy. Yet, we are blessed to know that we are not alone. If we believe in what God's Word teaches us about ourselves, and others, we know that we are fearfully and wonderfully made, Ps 139: 14. We know that no weapon made against us will prosper, Isaiah 54: 17. We know that all things work together for our good, Romans 8: 28. The question is not if it is so, but rather do we *believe* it is so. That is what this book is trying to help us understand. And if we believe that there is a God who loves us, who planned our lives a long time ago in eternity past, and who wants nothing but the best for us, how are we to live in this present age that provides more confusion than it provides answers, that offers temporary, quick "solutions" for deep seated problems, and places bandages on diseases that it just is not able to find cures for?

My thanks to my husband, Steve, who has provided unwavering support to me in my search for the truths that I will attempt to unveil in this work. I also want to recognize my first husband, also named Steve, who was equally supportive and loving and encouraged me to be my very best. Unfortunately, his life was cut short by cancer, but his legacy continues as I want to devote this book to both my Steves. I am truly doubly blessed by both of you, and I am eternally grateful for that.

Introduction

When I was about three years old, I had a severe infection in my throat, and had to spend two weeks in a children's hospital in my home town in Tampere, Finland. I do remember the doctor who sentenced me there, Dr. Ottila. Before him, I had been checked out by a doctor named Poyhonen. I was really angry. I was not sick, or at least not *that* sick. Mother took me by the hand as we walked up the spiral steps of the old hospital. "Mom, you cannot leave your little darling in this place," I pleaded as we walked up the stern looking spiral stairs to the second floor of the hospital. Well, I guess she did not feel that she had any choice in the matter. She had been caring for me at home for some time. She felt I was truly ill. So did the doctor.

I remember lying down in crib with metal slats that was used for my bed, looking out the window at the tall pine trees outside, and trying to figure out how I could escape from the miserable hospital room by climbing out the window, slinging myself from the window sill like Tarzan to the outstretched tree branches waiting for me out there. Perhaps I could somehow get out of these prison bars and make my escape! It was a wild idea, but I remember entertaining it quite a bit during the lonely hours I spent so isolated and alone. Parents were not allowed to stay with their children, but were allowed to come in daily. My parents came to see me every day, which was a huge highlight in my days there. They always brought me some little treat to pick up my spirits. I truly felt like this was a prison sentence to me. I hated the place with all my heart. The nurses were not nice. They did not respect the privacy of their young charges, or show any real care for us. They treated us more like objects rather than people. I remember the embarrassment I felt when they had us all, boys and girls alike, flip on our bellies so that they could crudely take our rectal temperatures in broad view of each other!

One day, we were told to all line up to go down to the basement for chest x-rays. I thought that was a crazy idea, especially when I realized that the basement floors were made of unfinished cement and were cold. We were not given any kind of slippers to wear. All of us kids were supposedly ill, but we had to stand in line waiting for our turn barefoot in the cold basement. Even to my three-year-old brain, that was insanity! I believe the x-rays were to rule out tuberculosis. Well, I did not have that, thankfully.

Even today, I still have some of those feelings of recognizing the inaptitude of our collective health care system, the unnecessary and often intrusive protocols, and the lack of respect for the individual's rights, even as a three-year-old child! And perhaps, most of all, the outrageous costs, at least in the United States. We often cannot change the circumstances we find ourselves in any more than a three-year-old girl could convince the doctors or those in charge to improve the care of the young patients placed in their care. My voice had no impact. My cries were never even registered. However, we do have a powerful God in heaven who hears our cries for justice and fairness, and who also knows suffering and pain in a much, much deeper sense than we can even imagine in the hands of those who did not know better, but should have. This was Jesus.

Today, we still struggle with many issues that seemingly make no sense. Why do we have so much violence in our cities? How come road rage often leads to murder and mayhem? Why do people have guns in their homes believing that they are protected when study after study shows that owning a gun puts the owner at much higher risk of being killed by a gun, than a non-gun owner? Not to mention the much higher risk of committing suicide. Why do we continue to punish people who kill by killing them as if that was a lesson they needed to learn? This makes absolutely no sense. What has happened to our sense of justice, compassion, truth, and righteousness? Why does our legal system appear to favor one race over another in its proceedings?

What about the growing crisis of drug addiction? Countless lives are shattered by the illusion that substances can offer lasting joy or fulfillment. But this, too, is a lie. Rather than healing, drugs only deepen the wounds—magnifying pain, destroying potential, and enslaving those lured by the promise of escape.

Racial tensions have reached an all-time high at a time when we are supposed to be more tolerant of differences than ever. The more we talk about racial equality, the further it seems to be out of our reach.

And how do we continue to allow the murder of the innocent pre-born babies in the womb by cutting them up limb by limb, and suctioning them out like something bad, something cancerous. They have not done anything wrong. All they are doing is growing to be the children of God He created them to be. Why do we punish them for the choices their parents have made?

Yet others go through painful efforts year after year trying to conceive that one precious little baby, the fulfillment of their hopes and dreams, and spending money they often do not have to make that dream a reality, sometimes succeeding, but often not. These are dichotomies that our modern world is grappling with. It is senseless. It is cruel. It is unjust.

Promiscuity, sexual violence, and gender confusion are on our daily news feed today. Where is God in all this? The God who created a man and a woman to be holy, to exist in special covenant relationship with each other, being one flesh, Genesis 1: 27, 2: 24.

God is a good and faithful Father, loving us with an everlasting love that surpasses our understanding. He cares for us in ways we may never fully grasp—protecting, guiding, and standing as our defender against every scheme of the enemy. In return, He asks only that we place our trust in Him and in the redemptive plan He has lovingly set in motion for our salvation.

As we look at life from a biblical perspective, we cannot help but wonder how God sees our world today. If Jesus were among us now, how would He address today's troubling issues?

When we look at the Scriptures today to begin our study on the significance of protecting life in all its forms, being pro-life in the deepest sense of the word, we need the guidance of the Holy Spirit so that our lives can reflect the glory of our God. Jesus told us that without Him, we can do nothing, John 15: 5. So as we launch on this journey of learning, we will humbly surrender our thoughts, words, and actions to His guidance in order to bring Him glory in everything we do. Let us pray this prayer:

Our Father in heaven, please guide us through Your Word to know the truth that is only found in You. We surrender our thoughts, our intellect, our preconceived ideas, our dearly held beliefs on the altar of Your holiness so that You and You alone will guide us to the truth of these significant and important topics. Help us to be clear and honest, and to diligently seek Your face as we strive to do Your will in everything we say and do. Fill our hearts with compassion, understanding, and grace as we explore Your Word. To You alone be all the glory. Amen.

Chapter One: The Origins of Life

"Woe to those who call evil good, and good evil, who put darkness for light, and light for darkness, who put bitter for sweet and sweet for bitter."

Isaiah 5:20 NIV.

In this era of expanding knowledge and technology, we are faced with many questions that have to do with the fundamental values that shape our beliefs, behaviors, and views. Some of the most crucial of those have to do with life itself. What is the value of human life? When does life begin? Is it morally right to end one's life when faced with a terminal illness or unbearable pain? Does the Bible support a pacifistic world view? How are we to respond to the violence we see in our society today? These, and many questions like them, can find their answers in the pages of the Bible if we prayerfully and carefully look at them.

Life is our most precious gift. Without life, we would not be able to ask these questions, or even inhale our next breath! Life is sacred. In Genesis 2: 7 we are told that the "Lord God formed the man from the dust of the ground and breathed into his nostrils the breath of life." In Jeremiah 1: 5, we learn that God knew us before He even "formed us in the womb". God has an eternal plan for each and every one of His created beings. He knew us and loved us even before we were fully formed in our mother's womb! In fact, He knew us even before we were conceived. This is because He knows the end from the beginning. He is not bound by our concept of time, but lives outside our perceived reality. Because of this foreknowledge, God was able to proclaim to Abraham that he would be the father of many nations, Genesis 17: 4, although Abraham had not yet had any offspring at all!

I often think of our reality as a fish bowl. The fish that are in the bowl do not know what is outside their bowl. They have no experience with the room where the bowl is placed, or its furnishings. They may see glimpses of a table and chairs, some book shelves, a couch, or a picture on the wall. However, they do not know what those things are used for, and they certainly have no experience in taking advantage of their comforts or even beauty. All their little universe consists of is the watery bowl that they have been placed in.

That is their known universe. They do not grasp the concept of time, but they know how to grasp food. Their little brains can handle the challenges they face in their "universe", but the outside world is not only foreign to their experience, but it is also down right lethal. They cannot live outside of their little universe for more than a few moments.

Just as a fish in a bowl cannot comprehend the world beyond its watery confines, we, too, are limited in our understanding of the vast, uncharted universe that surrounds us. God has placed us on this earth, providing for our needs, loving and protecting us. Yet even with our most advanced technologies, we catch only fleeting glimpses of the cosmos beyond. Even closer to home, the intricate design of our own bodies remains largely a mystery. Our immune system fights off countless unseen invaders each day, our liver detoxifies our blood while performing dozens of other vital functions, and our hearts beat rhythmically through an astonishing electrical system. Enzymes and muscles work in perfect harmony to break down food and sustain life—processes we barely comprehend. And yet, while we struggle to grasp even these details, God knows every aspect of the vast universe and the microscopic world within us. Most remarkably, He does so without ever losing sight of us, His beloved children.

Jesus taught us that He came so that we may have life and have it to the full, or abundantly, John 10:10. God does not want us to just exist, but He wants us to thrive. John also tells us that Jesus was life and that life was the light of men, John 1:4. Life in this world is a gift, and if we accept Christ as the Savior of the world, the Lamb of God, this life will usher us into our eternal home in heaven, as described in the book of Revelation.

"The thief comes only to steal and kill and destroy" (John 10:10, NIV). Too often, we forget that the enemy of our souls—the devil—is relentlessly working to tear us down. He seeks to steal our joy, kill our hope, and destroy our trust in a loving God and His promises.

His sole objective is to derail God's plan by planting seeds of doubt, fear, anxiety, pride, and division in our hearts. We live in a world where chaos and deception are his tools, and where a culture that often glorifies death overshadows the sanctity of life. I call this the "culture of death"—a force woven into entertainment, laws, leadership, traditions, and ever-shifting societal norms. It even infiltrates our personal ideologies when they stray from the firm foundation of Scripture, particularly the teachings of Jesus. But we must not allow the enemy's schemes to take root. Instead, we are called to let the Word of God dwell in us richly (Colossians 3:16), standing firm in His truth and light.

Let us go back to the beginning of Genesis to see what we find there.

Life is a gift. It is not something we planned ourselves. It was God's idea. Genesis 1: 26 says: *"Let us make man in our own image, in our likeness."* NIV. The word "man" here does not only refer to the male gender, but it refers to all of mankind, including women and children.

Furthermore, after God had created Adam and Eve, He blessed them and told them to be fruitful and increase in number, verse 28. God said it was not good for man to be alone, and therefore He created woman. Life is meant to be lived in community.

After God had completed His creation, He noted that it was "very good", Genesis 1: 31. God does good work. He does not create failures. We may sometimes struggle with the idea that we are indeed the children of a Heavenly King, and that all His works are wonderful. He did not create us by mistake. We are a part of His wonderful plan. Even when we fail to live our lives according to the principles God gave us in His Word, we are still valuable to Him, we are still loved by Him, and we are still His most precious creation!

From what we just read, we learn that:

1. Life is a gift. Life as God intended it was free for Adam and Eve to enjoy. There were no strings attached. The whole creation was theirs to explore, nurture, and maintain. Every green thing was food for them. There was no death. There was no sickness. There were no hurts, no pain. There were no bad words, no bad attitudes, no bad days —. Just communion with the Creator in the most beautiful setting we can ever imagine.

2. All life originates with God (Genesis 1: 11-27) Life did not happen by random accident. It is not the result of millions of years of natural selection. It was created by God by His word. "*In the beginning was the Word, and the Word was with God, and the Word was God. He was with God in the beginning. Through Him, all things were made; without Him, nothing was made that has been made. In Him was life, and that life was the light of men.*"John 1: 1-4 NIV. This is talking about Jesus. He was the life that existed from the very beginning.

3. Life produces unity (they become <u>one flesh</u> (Genesis 2: 24)

4. Life produces abundance and increase (Genesis 1:28)

5. Life is best lived in communion, or community, with others (Genesis 2:18)

6. Life provides man with meaningful and fulfilling work (Genesis 2: 15)

7. Life includes a blessing from God (Genesis 1: 28)

8. Life is good; God does not create junk (Genesis. 1:31)

9. From this, we can deduce that God, who gives life is good.

However, it did not take long for the good plans that God had for humanity to take an ugly turn. In chapter 3, we read about the opposite of life, death. Adam and Eve fell into disobedience to God. They failed to obey the one limitation on their freedom in the garden of Eden, or paradise, by believing a lie that was presented to them by the serpent, or the devil. The result of their disobedience was death. They had been deceived, duped by a slithering creature given voice by Satan himself. This death was immediately expressed as fear, shame, and blame. It later resulted in physical death, that was inevitable. This physical death would ultimately mean separation from the Creator, spending eternity alienated from the One who created us for communion with Himself. Furthermore, it resulted in the death of all of creation, including the animals that Adam was told to name in chapter 2 verse 19. The beautiful world created by God for mankind's joy and the pleasure of the Creator was now spiraling towards ultimate chaos.

From this we learn that:

1. Death was a *choice* made by man, (Genesis 2: 16-17).

2. Death was a result of disobedience, (Genesis 3:6)

3. Death was brought on by unbelief and deception, believing a lie, (Genesis 3: 4-5)

4. Death caused immediate shame, fear, and blaming others, (Genesis 3: 7-13).

5. Death caused the death of all the animals too, (Genesis 3:21).

6. Death caused a curse with painful labor, sickness, and suffering. Work was no longer pleasurable. Instead, it became toil, (Genesis 3: 6-19).

7. Death brought in division, jealousy, and murder, (Genesis 4).

8. Death brought in separation, (Genesis 3:23).

9. Death is the antithesis of God's will for us.

    In Romans 6:23, we read that *"the wages of sin is death."* NIV.

    Because of our sinful state, God sent us a Savior, Jesus Christ, so that through His death, we could be restored to fellowship with the Father. Christ died on the cross to forever destroy death, 2 Timothy 1: 10. He paid the price for our failures in the face of the most holy God. Because of Christ, death no longer rules over us. In fact, He promised that whoever lives and believes in Him will never die, John 11:26.

> The apostle John writes: *"In Him (Christ) was life, and that life was the light of men. The light shines in the darkness, but the darkness has not understood it", John 1: 4-5, NIV. "Through Him all things were made; without Him nothing was made that has been made,"*

John 1:3. NIV

> Jesus put it this way: *"I am the way, and the truth, and the life. No one comes to the Father except through me,"*

John 14: 6. NIV

Jesus is our life, in other words. If we know Him, we have life. Without Him, we have nothing, and we can do nothing. Life is essential for everything. We can identify planets, solar systems, and galaxies, but have yet to find any signs of life on any of them. As far as we know, the planets are dead. They have no life in them, and do not have the prerequisites that are required even for the most elementary forms of life. In Christ, however, we have life in this world, and the one to come, which is our heavenly home.

So if we agree that life is precious, and a prerequisite for existence in this world, or as a philosopher might say, it is fundamental for our consciousness, or awareness of self and others, we may want to take a closer look at the entire issue of life. If we did not have life, we could not argue about its significance. We could not present our opinions, voice our doubts, present counterpoints, or even form the thoughts required to have any kind of a view on the matter at all. It would be totally irrelevant as we would not be alive. The breath of

Life that God breathed on us in Genesis 2:7 is what makes us living, breathing, thinking individuals. This is what God had in mind when He created us. He did not create us to be dead bodies with no thoughts, no function, no purpose. He created us to be His image bearers (Genesis 1: 26). We have been stamped by Him, the Creator of the universe, to represent Him on this earth. We have the unique responsibility to represent God in our lives. For many unbelieving people around us, we are the only gospel they will ever read. Do our lives reflect the glory of our heavenly Father? If not, how can we grow in our walk, and in our witness? Would it be by picking up our cross each and every day with humility and purpose? By caring for the physical, emotional, spiritual, and relational needs of those around us?

In Deuteronomy — 30:15, we read what God clearly stated to the people of Israel: *"See, I have set before you this day life and good, and death and evil."* NKJV. God makes it abundantly clear that life is what He intends to give us. Our choices sometimes lead us in another direction, and that direction is evil, and leads to death. This is what Adam and Eve chose in the Garden of Eden, and we all have made this same choice at one time or another. We probably make that choice every day in our actions and attitudes.

Furthermore, God gets more specific a few verses later. We read in Deuteronomy 30:19–20, *"This day I call heaven and earth as witnesses against you that I have set before you life and death, blessings and curses. Now choose life, so that you and your children may live and that you may love the Lord your God, listen to His voice, and hold fast to Him. For the Lord is your life, and He will give you many years in the land He swore to give to your fathers, Abraham, Isaac, and Jacob"* (NIV, underlining added).

Could God have expressed His desire towards us any more clearly than that? His desire is for us to prosper, and more than that. He wants us to be His representatives on this earth. He wants us to bear witness to His goodness and how His goodness can only be worked through us by faith in His forgiveness through Jesus Christ.

But before we go further into the study of God's word, let us take a few moments to review what the secular world might say about being pro-life.

The Urban Dictionary defines being pro-life as follows:

"The belief that all life is sacred and deserves to be protected. One who is truly pro-life will oppose capital punishment, war, poverty, and all forms of physical and mental torture. Such a person will see abortion as a tragedy for all involved, not a "reproductive right" to be celebrated, and will work to end abortion, not by force or intimidation, but by working to change the social and economic conditions that lead people to choose abortion."

While this definition may not fully satisfy those who oppose abortion under all circumstances—as many Bible-believing, born-again Christians do—it nonetheless serves as a meaningful starting point for deeper conversation. It highlights elements of the pro-life perspective that are often overlooked, dismissed, or deemed irrelevant in broader discussions. At its core, being pro-life means honoring and protecting all human life, from the moment of conception to its natural end. But it also extends beyond that: it involves safeguarding the environment we've been entrusted with, maintaining the delicate balance between humanity and the creation we are called to steward. It reflects a commitment to minimizing harm to all living beings under our care, and revering the life God has lovingly imparted to each one.

Unlike some critics would say, it does not make animals equal to humans. Animals are not equal to us, but they also suffer due to the choices we have made as fallen creatures. Animals were not created in the image of God. But they also are sentient beings that can sense pain, love, fear, rejection, depression, and even hope. Paul said it this way in his letter to the Romans: *"For we know that the whole creation groans and travails in pain together until now,* "Romans 8:22. KJV. If the whole creation indeed groans and travails, as Paul asserts, then these must be sentient beings! There is no other explanation. The dissonance we as humans have brought into God's beautiful creation echoes even in the entire created world, the same world that God told Adam to *"dress and keep"* in Genesis 2:15 KJV.

Caring about life includes caring for all living creatures, and the environment that provides us with nourishment and sustenance. In recent years, we have seen the devastation of wild fires in California, Colorado, and other states in the West. We have seen floods, hurricanes, and tornadoes of unforeseen strength and frequency in various areas. These, among other things, are caused by man's careless actions, which are taking a toll on natural resources, and causing changes in our polar caps, rising ocean levels, and previously unseen climactic patterns. Our planet is slowly heating up. We are like the frog in the pot of lukewarm water. It does not feel uncomfortable, and so it sits there even as the temperature rises to boiling. It is getting used to the heat. And eventually it dies before it realizes that it is time to get out of the boiling pot! May God keep us alert and aware of what is happening around us so we can be equipped to handle any situation through His word and power given to us.

In Psalm 102: 19-20, we read: *"The Lord looked down from His sanctuary on high, from heaven He viewed the earth, to hear the groans of the prisoners and release those condemned to death." NIV.*

This is an interesting passage in a psalm that appears to be written by an afflicted person who is pouring out his heart before the Lord. And God apparently shows him and his buddies mercy. It does not state whether the prisoners were incarcerated for a severe crime, or whether they were condemned to death due to being part of the wrong tribe or nation that had been defeated. Regardless of their guilt, God is willing to allow them to live.

In another psalm, we find David praying, after he had committed virtual murder by assigning Uriah in a position of almost certain death on the battle field to cover up his adulterous relationship with his wife, Bathsheba, in 2 Samuel 11. It reads in Psalm 51:14 *"Forgive me for shedding blood, O God who saves; then I will joyfully sing of your forgiveness."* (New Living Translation) The New International Version states it this way: *"Deliver me from the guilt of bloodshed, O God, you who are God my Savior, and my tongue will sing of your righteousness."*

So we understand that despite the frequent killings, wars, and even murders that are so graphically described in the Old Testament, and the laws that would condemn one to death following a murder, such as Genesis 9:6, there is a loving God who actually forgives even the most heinous deeds to those who sincerely repent and ask for forgiveness.

In Genesis 9: 6 we read: *"Whoever sheds the blood of man, by man shall his blood be shed, for in the image of God has God made man."* NIV. This command was given to Noah after the flood, long before the law was given through Moses in Exodus. Jesus, on the other hand stated:

"You have heard that it was said, 'An eye for an eye, and a tooth for a tooth.' But I tell you, Do not resist an evil person. If someone strikes you on the right cheek, turn to him the other also. And if someone wants to sue you and take take your tunic, let him have your cloak as well. If someone forces you to go one mile, go with him two miles."

Matthew 5: 38-41. NIV.

The foundation of the pro-life movement can, in fact, be traced back to Genesis 9:6, where we're reminded that humanity holds immeasurable value because we are made in the image of God. This divine imprint gives each life sacred worth. If we were to take the Old Testament command literally—that those who take a life must forfeit their own—and apply it alongside Jesus' teaching that even speaking ill of a brother is akin to murder, few of us would be left standing. His standard is impossibly high, revealing not just the sanctity of life, but our deep need for grace.

In Exodus 23:7 we are told *"Keep yourself far from false matter; do not kill the innocent and righteous."* NKJV. In Proverbs 24:11 we read: *"Rescue those who are unjustly sentenced to die; save them as they stagger to their death."* NLT. Yet, in the United States, we have put to death a great number of innocent people who did not have the means to defend themselves properly in court. This includes many individuals of color and many who were too poor to afford proper defense. We have thus become guilty of shedding innocent blood! That is a travesty.

In the following chapters we will examine several core issues regarding the pro-life stand and what the Bible teaches concerning each of these. This is not meant to create a politically volatile atmosphere charged with partisan or divisive views. This is to help us understand the awesome love our Heavenly Father has towards us. How He has loved us long before we were *"knit together in our mother's womb"* Psalm 139: 13 to paraphrase the verse from NIV, and that love has never failed us, and never will. God is the same yesterday, today, and forever. His love and His purpose for us are from eternity past. And they reach far beyond the grave.

Chapter Two: Righting Wrongs the Right Way

Speak up for those who cannot speak for themselves, for the rights of all who are destitute. Speak up and judge fairly; defend the rights of the poor and needy."

Proverbs 31:8 NIV.

"Blessed are the merciful for they will be shown mercy,"

Matthew 5: 7 NIV.

"I was in prison and you came to visit me",

Matthew 25:36 NIV.

"For to us a child is born, to us a son is given, and the government will be on his shoulders. And he will be called Wonderful Counselor, Mighty God, Everlasting Father, Prince of Peace. Of the increase of his government and peace there will be no end."

Isaiah 9: 6-7. NIV.

SINIKKA PEMBER-COULTER

Two men, Marcellus Williams, 55, in Missouri and Travis Mullis, 38, in Texas, were executed on September 24, 2024. And on Friday, in Carolina, there was the first execution in that state in over 13 years.

Marcellus Williams was executed despite doubts of his guilt with both the victim's family and the prosecutor's office that secured his murder conviction, calling for the execution to be stopped. In addition, a petition calling for the execution to be stopped gained 1.5 million signatures. Despite all this, the Missouri and US Supreme Courts and Gov. Mike Parson allowed the execution to take place.

Travis Mullis was executed by the State of Texas for the tragic and horrific murder of his three-month-old child on January 29th, 2008—a crime he committed in response to the child's persistent crying. It was, without question, a deeply disturbed and devastating act. Yet even in the face of such undeniable guilt, we must confront a challenging truth: a person's life does not lose its value, even when they have committed grave wrongs. As followers of Christ, we believe that only Jesus has the power to erase sin and redeem the soul. To add to His redemptive work, the act of state-sanctioned execution is not only unnecessary—it stands in tension with the heart of the gospel we profess to uphold.

Here is a well-known passage of Isaiah we are introduced to the Person of God. He is said to be wise counselor, a mighty God, a Father who lasts forever, and a Prince of Peace. WOW! That is quite a description of the divine nature and the dimensions of the godhead! He is wise, He is strong, He is eternal. He is full of Peace, in Hebrew "Shalom," "which also describes the sense of total well-being, safety, and wholeness."

So, what does all of this have to do with the sanctity of life here on earth, one might ask. We know that once are in heaven, there are no more tears, no more struggles, no more pain or sorrow. *"He will wipe every tear from their eyes. There will be no more death or mourning or crying or pain, for the old order of things has passed away."* Revelation 21:4. NIV.

This tells us that the intent of God towards man is only good. He is our loving Father. He is also our Good Shepherd who is deeply grieved if even one of his sheep goes astray, John 10:11.

"But if we walk in the light as He is in the light, we have fellowship with one another, and the blood of Jesus, His Son, purifies us from all sin."

1 John 1:7. NIV.

If we walk with Jesus, we have fellowship with one another. That means we will not have violent intentions. We will not have a desire to do evil or harm our brothers or sisters. We will be filled with His Love. We will live in forgiveness and charity. *"Anyone who claims to be in the light but hates his brother is still in darkness. Whoever loves his brother lives in the light."* 1 John 2: 9-10. NIV.

In the Old Testament there are many laws having to do with death as the punishment for sin. The death penalty was to be applied for a number or crimes and infractions, not just crimes of murder. In Leviticus 20: 9, we read that if anyone curses his father or mother, he must be put to death. Anyone caught in adultery must be put to death, verse 10. In verse 13, we read that people engaging in homosexual behavior must be put to death, verses 15,16. And anyone who is a medium or spiritist must be put to death, verse 27. There are also various commands concerning other types of sexual behavior that are not permissible, that in many cases, requires the death penalty. In addition, there are a number of other ordinances that have to do with priestly behavior and sacrifices in the tabernacle and breaking God's commands often resulted in being being cut off from the people, as in Leviticus 17: 3-4, and again in verses 8-10. Anyone offering their children as a sacrifice to Molek, a pagan god, must be stoned, Leviticus 20: 2. If a priest's daughter becomes a prostitute, she must be burned in the fire, Leviticus 21: 9. In Leviticus 24: 10-16 we read of God's punishment of a man who blasphemed the Lord's name. He was to be stoned to death. So was anyone else who committed this sin.

We also read in Numbers 15 about a man who was gathering wood on the Sabbath day. After Moses inquired of the Lord what to do with this man, the Lord ordered him to be stoned to death by the whole community outside the camp, Numbers 15: 32-36. Again, in Deuteronomy 13: 1-13, we read about how anyone who tries to entice a person to follow other, pagan gods, even if it is their own brother, son, daughter, wife, or closest friend, must be stoned to death.

The Old Testament offers an unflinching view of God's justice, where the consequences of sin were often swift and severe. One striking example is the rebellion of Korah, son of Izhar, as recorded in Numbers 16:1–35. Korah, along with 250 prominent leaders, challenged the authority of Moses and Aaron—an act of defiance that ended in divine judgment. The earth opened and swallowed Korah, Dathan, and Abiram, along with their families and possessions, while fire from the Lord consumed the remaining rebels. In this dramatic display, God revealed not only His unmatched power but also His unwavering standard for righteousness.

We find that according to the law of Moses, there are lots of reasons where the death penalty could be applied, as we see here. Sometimes God degreed it, at other times, as we see in the judgment against Korah and his followers, God Himself took justice in His own hands. It would be very difficult and extremely merciless to try to apply these laws in our legal system today. Can you imagine what our society would look like if all adulterers or homosexuals, or everyone who blasphemes the Lord's name, or worships other idols, such as money, sports, sex, violence, fame, and the like, were condemned to death, as an example? How about if anyone collecting firewood on a Shabbath was stoned to death? There would hardly be any people left alive on this planet! So now the question is, does Jesus support these laws in the way they were presented.

In contrast, we read about Jesus' reaction when confronted with the woman accused of adultery in John 8. He did not ask, where the man committing the adultery was, so we can stone them both, as the law would have required. Instead, He waited a moment, bending down to draw something on the ground, apparently asking the Father to give Him the right words to say. He then straightened Himself up and told the crowd: *"If any of you is without sin, let him be the first to throw a stone at her,"* John 8: 7 NIV. Bang.

A heavy silence fell as, one by one, the accusers let their stones drop to the ground. Rather than reciting the law, Jesus shifted the focus entirely. He didn't condemn the woman—though her guilt was clear—but instead turned the spotlight onto her accusers, urging them to examine their own hearts in light of God's holiness. Even the Pharisees, known for their strict adherence to the law, couldn't claim innocence. In the presence of God's perfect Lamb—the only one without sin—they were stripped of their self-righteousness. Convicted by the truth, they walked away. For the reality remains: we are all guilty. To break even one commandment is to stand condemned by the entire law.

Jesus did not excuse the woman or her behavior. He acknowledged the sin as sin. Jesus did not whitewash the action. He did not try to overturn the law. Neither did He question whether the law was justified. He had a better way of dealing with sin, than punishing the sinner with death. *"Woman, where are they? Has no one condemned you?"* John 8: 10 NIV, as one by one the stones fell with a thud on the sandy pavement and the men quietly retreated, leaving only Jesus and the woman standing there. *"No one, sir,"* she said. *Then Jesus replied with most liberating words imaginable: "Then neither do I condemn you. Go now and leave your life of sin."* NIV. It is comforting to know that once our accusers leave, Jesus is still there. He is always there to help us in our weaknesses. He loves us with an everlasting love. His mercies are new every morning! He will never leave, not forsake us.

"And what does the Lord require of you? To act justly, to love mercy, and to walk humbly with your God"

Micah 6: 8. NIV.

Why would Jesus say this, one might ask. The law was very clear. Jesus did follow the law, but He also acknowledged a *higher* law, the law of love and mercy. He also exposed the ethical dilemma of judging others. In the sermon on the mount, Christ teaches that we should not judge others: *"Why do you look at the speck of sawdust in your brother's eye and pay no attention to the plank in your own eye?,"* Matthew 7: 3. NIV. In talking with the Pharisees about the Sabbath and what that entailed, Jesus was defending His disciples, who had picked some heads of grain in the field as they were passing by. This, according to the Pharisees, was against the law. Jesus talked about the priests and how their duties required them to desecrate the Sabbath rules in the temple and yet were innocent. He then stated something very important: "If you had known what these words mean, *'I desire mercy, not sacrifice,' you would not have condemned the innocent."* Matthew 12: 7. NIV

So if God in His great mercy forgives us our sins, and casts them as far as the East is from the West, Psalm 103: 12, the who are we to judge someone, and by doing so possibly send them to eternal hell fire, if they have not, as of yet, come to know the Lord as their Savior? On the other hand, if they <u>have</u> come to know Jesus as Lord and Savior, they are then our brother or sister. Why would be want to condemn them to death? Neither scenario makes any sense if you really think about it.

As believers who trust the Lord for our eternal salvation, in other words, we trust that by believing in Jesus' death and resurrection, and the remission of all of our sins on the cross, we will inherit eternity with Him, it would seem odd that we would want to deprive a criminal, no matter how horrendous the crime they may have committed, of the possibility to accept Christ and be saved for all eternity! God's desire is for all to come to a saving knowledge of Christ. In other words, by endorsing the taking of life of an unrepentant criminal, we not only deprive them of life in this world, but much more seriously, we also deprive them of the possibility of finding forgiveness and restoration in Christ! God forbid we should ever stand in the way of anyone coming to Christ. Instead, we should do everything we can to give the gospel to those who are in prison, those whose hearts are broken. *"He (God) is patient with you not wanting anyone to perish, but everyone to come to repentance."* 2 Peter 3: 9. NIV.

While we can—and should—recognize actions that are wrong or sinful according to God's Word, it's essential not to confuse judging behavior with condemning the person. God hates sin, yet He loves the sinner—a distinction we're called to uphold. In the same way, we're right to feel anger at injustice, to speak out when individuals or communities are exploited or denied their rights. This is righteous anger—not aimed at the people themselves, but at the wrongs they commit. Still, we must be cautious in judging others, remembering that only God truly knows the heart. As we seek wisdom, the Holy Spirit offers discernment, helping us navigate these complexities with grace. (We'll explore the Spirit's role in more depth shortly.)

It is simply incongruous to speak the truth about the value of the life of an unborn child in the womb, to extoll God's great creativity, and purpose, and yet in the next breath to condemn someone to death by electrocution, or lethal injection, or some other brutal, inhumane means, because they have broken one of God's commandments, and also broken the law of the land. That soul that now stands condemned, naked, and helpless, was also once a baby in his or her mother's womb, whether wanted or not, whether planned for or not. Still, an amazing masterpiece of God's infinite creativity, still a soul with nearly unlimited potential. As Christians, who are we to judge a person? Do we expect that unborn baby that we are protecting, and rightly so, to live a sinless life, one that never grieves their mother or father, never hurts another person, never says a gross word? That would be a preposterous assumption, and yet we treat some individuals as "innocent" and others as "guilty." This is a very unbiblical proposition. The Bible clearly states that _all have sinned and come short of the glory of God,_ Romans 3: 23. NIV. What the Bible means by "all" is actually everybody, you and I included.

The Bible teaches us clearly that we are not to judge others, as by judging others, we heap judgment on our own heads, because none of us is guiltless, Matthew 7: 1-2. The standard of behavior Jesus presented to the crowds in the Sermon of Mount far exceeds the 613 commandments found in the Torah and other writings that the scribes and Pharisees so diligently tried to obey, and even more diligently tried to get others to obey. In Matthew 5: 21-22, Jesus defines "murder" as a sin of the heart, rather than just a physical assault against someone else. This does not mean that murder is not a serious crime. It most certainly is. However, Jesus made the point that many of us who have never committed such an atrocity in real life, may have harbored hatred or vengeance against another in our hearts. We may have used bad language against someone in anger. Perhaps, if given the chance, we might have even wanted to punch someone really hard, which might have caused them to die. Regardless, in God's eyes, hatred of a brother or sister is equal to murder. This is truly a high bar that Jesus sets before us. How can anyone meet this standard?

The truth is, no one can. Only by faith in Jesus Christ, the living God who became flesh for us so that He could take away our guilt and shame, can we be freed from the guilt and penalty for our sins. So, to persist in claiming that a criminal accused of murder should be punished by death, in other words, by removal from the land of the living, seems very contradictory to the way Jesus would view this person, and the righteous judgment against them. If all indeed have sinned, as we learned earlier, then all also can have access to God's redemptive plan.

"For God so loved the world that He gave His one and only Son, that whoever believes in Him, shall not perish but have eternal life. For God did not send His Son to the world to condemn the world, but to save the world through Him. Whoever believes in Him is not condemned, but whoever does not believe stands condemned already because he has not believed in the name of God's one and only Son."

John 3: 16-18. NIV.

This is what happened to a Texas prisoner named Karla Faye Tucker, who was on death row in the Gatesville Women's prison in Texas for a murder she had committed under influence of drugs. While in prison, she became a believer through someone taking her through *Experiencing God,* a Bible course that teaches a radically God-centered way of life. She was so impacted by the truths presented in the book that she began to teach other inmates on death row. Because of her testimony, so many women came to know Jesus that they renamed their the death row Life Row, because they came to know true life in Christ. Her crime was a heinous act for sure, but her testimony impacted the whole nation, and touched the world. Still, the governor of Texas refused her request for clemency, and she was executed for her crime. This was tragedy beyond belief.

How can we judge her crime to be greater than that of many of us who have done evil things to others? According to Jesus, to hate someone, or to call them a fool, is already worthy of judgment, and even eternal hell fire, Matthew 5: 21-22.

If we're honest, most of us have been guilty of hatred—whether in word or thought—at some point in our lives. So, who are we to decide which hateful actions merit the death penalty? Capital punishment doesn't heal wounds or restore what's been lost. It offers no true comfort to the grieving and perpetuates the illusion that one wrong can somehow be balanced by another. But only Jesus took the death penalty and turned it into redemption. To claim someone must "pay" for their crime through death is, in essence, to diminish the power of the cross. Christ already paid the ultimate price—once and for all—to set us free from sin and proclaim liberty to the captives, just as Isaiah 61:1 foretold. He is the true and final fulfillment of the law.

When the State takes over and punishes a criminal for the very same action that the criminal committed, they become guilty of the very same act that they now condemn someone to death for. This makes no sense. It only perpetuates the *culture of death,* not respect for life. Society should set an example of good, decent behavior, and respect for the life of self and others. This type of punishment erodes societal values and inadvertently makes killing people an acceptable practice.

As believers in Christ, we are to proclaim liberty to the captives, not death, by an inconceivably cruel panel of judges or jury, who, based on often very faulty and politically or racially biased information, come to the conclusion that this type of penalty is in order.

Many people believe that death is the right punishment if someone has committed murder. To them, this represents equal justice. While each situation, or crime is different, we must never underestimate the fact that a state sanctioned killing has far more psychological implications than even the most heinous murder in open society. How can we say this, you might ask. Isn't murdering someone the worst thing anyone can do to someone else? Yes, this is true. However, when someone is being tortured or killed, there is always the hope of escape or relief of some kind. Perhaps my cries are heard by someone. Perhaps I can fight myself out of this horrific situation. Perhaps I can convince my attacker to retreat. Perhaps I can pray, and God will give me supernatural strength and protection. Perhaps… The murder victim always has the law on their side, not against them. There is still hope. This hope is precious, and life altering. When we legalize murder, we have taken away the person's hope for redemption. We have essentially counted them unworthy of living.

A person condemned to death by state sanctioned execution has no such hope. It is as if they have been rejected by society as "unfit" to even live, unworthy of participating in the human community. This may be the way the world would look at a criminal. Many would cry for revenge. Their anger and hatred cannot be satisfied by anything other than seeing the perpetrator of the crime dead. And even that does not heal them from their anger and self-imposed misery. It will not bring their loved one back to life. The fact remains that God made us for fellowship, not for retaliation. God assures us, in His Word, that He is a just God and will not let evil go unpunished. We are assured of this in many parts of the Bible, and Nahum 1: 3 is just one of them.

As believers in Christ and His redemptive work of salvation, no one is to be discarded as worthless. Christ took upon Himself the guilt and sins of us all. To claim that this is not enough, the blood of Christ is not enough to cleanse us of all our sins, is to actually blaspheme the work of Christ.

"Blessed is the one whose transgressions are forgiven, whose sins are covered. Blessed is the one whose sin the Lord does not count against them and in whose spirit is no deceit. When I kept silent, my bones wasted away through my groaning all day long. For day and night your hand was heavy on me; my strength was sapped as in the heat of summer. Then I acknowledged my sin to you and did not cover up my iniquity. I said 'I will confess my transgressions to the Lord.' And you forgave the guilt of my sin."

Psalm 32:1-5 NIV.

On October 6, 2006, tragedy struck the quiet village of Nickel Mines in Lancaster County, Pennsylvania. A gunman entered the West Nickel Mines School, a one-room Amish schoolhouse, carrying a 9mm handgun, a 12-gauge pump-action shotgun, and a Ruger bolt-action rifle. He took the lives of five young girls, wounded five others, and then turned the gun on himself.

In the face of such unimaginable loss, the Amish community responded not with rage, but with radical forgiveness. Even the families of the victims expressed sorrow—not only for their own loss, but for the shooter, Charles Roberts. They grieved that he had taken his own life, fearing he may not have had the chance to repent and seek salvation. It was a deeply Christ-like response—one that demonstrated the power of grace in the darkest of moments.

Amish faith is grounded in the teachings of Jesus to love our enemies, reject revenge, and leave vengeance in the hands of God. As a father who lost a daughter in the schoolhouse said, "Forgiveness means giving up the right to revenge."

A person who is given a life sentence, as opposed to the death penalty, as Cain was by God after he killed his brother Abel in Genesis 4, may be exonerated if new evidence, such as advanced DNA samples, prove that the person was, in fact, innocent. Once a person has been murdered by the State, there is no recourse. The innocent person has died for something they did not do. This alone should cause us to oppose the death penalty, if nothing else did. Our legal system, although expensive and fair in principle, is often biased based on circumstantial evidence. Race plays a huge role in how justice is administered. This is not right. Hardly a week goes by that we do not hear of another death row inmate who has been exonerated due to lack of evidence, or new evidence implicating someone else. As Christians, we have to be extremely careful not to judge, even in these circumstances. We must presume innocence until proved guilty beyond a reasonable doubt.

Cain is an example of someone receiving a life sentence, not the death penalty. Cain murdered his own brother in Genesis 4, and this was the very first murder in the history of man. God's penalty for Cain's murder was his separation from everyone he knew and held dear for the rest of his life. In those days there were no judges, no prisons, no laws to govern behavior. Yet, God has placed in each person a conscience that directs them to know right from wrong. Therefore, Cain knew that what he did was a sin, a horrific crime. He had acted out of jealousy, impulsively, but tried to cover up for his brutality by saying he was not his brother's keeper. Indeed, he was not. He was his murderer!

Cain's response to God after this judgment was pronounced to him is highly indicative of the implications and severity of this life-long separation for Cain.

He stated in Genesis 4: 13 *"My punishment is too great for me to bear! You have banished me from the land and from your presence; you have made me a wandering fugitive. All who see me will try to kill me."* NLT.

I believe God created this precedent to show us that ultimately His focus is not on vengeance or the method of paying an eye for an eye, or tooth for a tooth, a life for a life, but He actually protects life. This law of <u>protecting</u> life, while also providing appropriate punishment, preceded the law given by Moses, and even the order given to Noah after the flood. This must have been on God's heart all along.

In response, we actually see God telling specifically that He <u>would not allow anyone to kill Cain</u>. He would put a mark on Cain to warn anyone who might try to kill him. In other words, God made certain that no one would take the death penalty into their own hands against Cain! That really shows what God thought of the justice of the death penalty, doesn't it? To live with his guilt for the rest of his life, was more than enough punishment for Cain. It should be more than enough for us also, who have been sealed by the blood of Christ, and whose sins have been forgiven and cast as far as the East is from the West. If we want vengeance against the perpetrator of a crime, and thereby support the killing of the murderer, we are trampling on territory that belongs to God alone. In Deuteronomy 32: 35, we read how God claims the exclusive authority over <u>all</u> vengeance. This mostly had to do with capital offenses. How much more should this principle be applied to other types of infractions? Paul answers that question in Romans 12: 17-21. Paul reiterated the principle of God's vengeance by quoting that very Old Testament passage. But he also added *"Do not avenge yourselves, beloved, but leave room for God's wrath."* KJV This is a reference to God's righteous anger and judgement. He then continues: *"Do not be overcome by evil, but overcome evil with good."* KJV.

The only death penalty that ever accomplished anything as far as making things right, was the death penalty that put Christ on a wooden cross. He was innocent of any sin, and yet He carried the burden of all of our sins, past, present, and future. God is omniscient, and He knew that day that you and I would be inhabiting this planet at this time, and that our walk would not always measure up to His perfect standard. So He sent His Son to die for the sins of the whole world, not just the Jewish people, for all time, not just those who were His contemporaries and those who had preceded Him. He died for every single person who has ever lived, or will live on this earth.

Even within prison walls, a life can still hold meaning and purpose. We live in the age of grace, not law—an era where restoration is possible. Stories like Karla's remind us that faith, hope, love, courage, and perseverance can bloom even in the bleakest circumstances. But for this redemptive work to unfold, the justice system must function not only to protect society and uphold the rights of victims, but also to offer dignity and hope to those who have committed even the most terrible crimes.

In many cases, society must step in as the parent figure—providing the structure, accountability, and compassion that many offenders never experienced growing up. As believers, we're called to stand in the gap—to offer reason where there is confusion, compassion where there is pain, and love where there has only been abandonment. In extending grace, we grow too. And through our love, others may witness the transforming power of redemption. After all, Jesus said we would be known not by our judgments, but by our love.

Moses is an example of someone who had committed murder, and was hoping that no one saw him as he covered up the body in the sand. When it turned out that his violent act had been seen, and that Pharaoh was trying to kill him as a result, he fled, Exodus 2: 11-15. You would think that this was the end of Moses' story. He had failed miserably by killing someone in a fit of anger, then trying to cover up his murder. It has been speculated that Moses thought this was the way God wanted him to free his people, the Israelites, from the oppression and slavery imposed on them by the Egyptians. He finally he fled from the justice of the land. He became a man wanted for murder, a fugitive. You would think that there was no hope for this man. How could he ever recover from this? His own conscience must have bothered him day and night. And yet God had a different plan for him. Ultimately, he would deliver the Hebrew nation out of bondage as God directed him, and he also guided them through forty years of wandering in the desert in search of their own homeland while providing this rebellious nation God's laws and directions.

We must always remember that our legal system is just as imperfect as the people who created it. If new evidence vindicates the defendant of the crime they are being convicted of, a person serving a life sentence can benefit from that truth being revealed, and can be set free. A dead person cannot be compensated for this wrong. Their fate on this earth has been sealed. And their eternity has also been determined.

These reflections may feel weighty—perhaps even uncomfortable—but we live in a world saturated with violence, and silence is no longer an option. As believers, we are called to be ready with an answer when others question the foundation of our faith. If we falter or contradict ourselves, the very people we are meant to reach with Christ's love will see only inconsistency—and walk away not just from us, but from the message of hope we convey.

Our convictions must be rooted in Scripture and lived out with integrity. We cannot claim to value life while turning a blind eye to the fate of those who have lost their way. If we are to truly follow Christ, we must uphold the fullness of His message—a message of justice, yes, but also of mercy, redemption, and unwavering love. Anything less falls short of the cross we are called to carry.

When Christ hung on the Roman cross, naked and beaten, suffering an unjust death penalty for us all in the hands of the Romans to palliate the Jewish leaders and the mob that had hailed Him as King only days earlier, He chose to forgive them all. He also forgave the sins of the criminal who was crucified next to him.

The cross was the most demeaning way of putting someone to death. The Jews were not allowed to use this horrific punishment. Roman citizens could not be subjected to such an inhumane execution either. The Jewish law only allowed stoning as a method of execution. In Galatians 3: 13, we read that Christ became a curse for us for it is written: *"Cursed is everyone who is hung on a tree."* NIV. By taking our sins on Himself, Christ actually became sin for us. It is hard to imagine what this all meant. God pouring out His wrath on His Son, the One He had called *"My Beloved Son, in whom I am well pleased,"* Matthew 3:17 ESV as He was being baptized by John the Baptist. How could God allow His beloved Son to be tortured and humiliated in such an incredibly brutal way? He had done nothing but preach the Kingdom of God, heal the sick, raise others from death, and feed thousands with a few loaves and fishes. What was His crime?

The cross tells us clearly that there is no justice in manmade systems. True, we are to honor those placed in authority and respect their decisions, but ultimate justice will be delivered at a much later point in God's timetable. Jesus taught about it in Matthew 25, and it is given central place in the events culminating in the establishment of Christ's rule on the earth for a thousand years, and even at the end of that when all the nations will be judged by God's standards of holiness. Every action, word, and even thought will be scrutinized and weighed. Even believers will be called to judgement of our actions, but for the believer, there is no longer a call for punishment. Instead, our actions, words, and intentions are measured for their effectiveness towards bringing God's kingdom on the earth. Jesus taught about this in His parable of the talents. For non-believers, a similar measure is used, but it is used for judgement, not for rewards, because they have rejected God's free offer of grace. But regardless of which group you find yourself in, the believers, or the unbelievers, your actions, words, and motives bear great weight in eternity.

Matthew 25:31–46 offers a vivid and sobering glimpse into the reality of coming judgment. True to His teaching style, Jesus uses relatable imagery—this time, the separation of sheep and goats. The sheep represent those who lived with compassion, often helping others instinctively, without seeking recognition. In contrast, the goats symbolize those who overlooked the needs around them, failing to act when they had the chance. Jesus draws a clear line between the two through their actions—or inactions—and reveals the eternal consequences that follow. This passage leaves no room to doubt Christ's deep desire to spare humanity from eternal separation, as stated plainly in verse 46. To dismiss the reality of life after death is not only to deceive others, but to deceive oneself.

Christ's sacrifice of Himself was for *us*. He loved us and gave Himself for us so that we would not have to bear the wrath of the Holy God. He did for us so we could have life eternal instead. In John 10:10 Jesus says that He came to give us life, and that we may have it more abundantly, as we mentioned earlier too. He did not come to the earth to be a "killjoy." He did not come to take away the pleasure of living. Instead, He came to show us a path that will lead to joy in this life, and an eternal communion with the Father once this life is over.

The Bible does not specify the crime committed by the man crucified alongside Jesus—he may have been a thief, a political rebel, or even a murderer. But to our Lord, the nature of his offense was not what mattered. In the midst of His own unimaginable suffering, Jesus offered the man something far greater than judgment: comfort, assurance, and the promise of paradise. That very day, the man was forgiven and welcomed into eternal life. What a Savior we have— one who forgives completely and unconditionally.

Shouldn't we strive to follow His example? Rather than casting off those who have broken society's laws, should we not seek to restore those who truly regret their actions? At the very least, we should offer them the chance for growth and redemption, even as they serve their sentences. Every life holds value—even one that has taken another. If we believe that murder is not a solution to conflict or envy, then how can we justify responding to it with more death? As followers of Christ, our role is not to condemn souls to eternal separation from God, but to extend grace, hope, and the opportunity for salvation—even to those who have fallen the furthest.

Not only did Christ forgive the criminal who was crucified with him, but he also asked God to forgive those who put Him on the cross! His forgiveness was boundless; it is up to us to accept His open invitation. We are given the opportunity to embrace Jesus' invitation, to wholeheartedly put our faith and trust in His grace. Jesus did not try to whitewash the crime that the criminal crucified next to Him had committed. He did not say it did not matter. Jesus always called "sin" sin, as in the famous passages of the Sermon on the Mount in Matthew 5: 21-22. Jesus' standard for what amounts to sin goes even deeper than that of the Mosaic law. In Matthew 5:27 Jesus taught concerning adultery. His definition includes the thoughts and intentions of the heart, the sin that *would* be committed should the opportunity present itself.

People who consider the death penalty to be a deterrent to crime should look at the statistics. Actually, the death penalty is often not feared by those who commit horrendous crimes. Many times, they consider their lives worthless. Their actions are often, although not always, a result of desperation, and depression, as we well as uncontrolled anger, which our society tends to only facilitate. To be condemned to live the rest of their lives in prison is often the far greater fear. Countries that do not have the death penalty generally have less violent crime than those that do.

Sometimes, we hear Romans 13:1-5 quoted as a justification for capital punishment. If governing authorities are tasked with keeping civil order by using a sword, which would be comparable to a pistol or other such weapon today, is that not justification for capital punishment? Absolutely not. What Paul is here referring to is the right of our earthly authorities to keep peace, maintain order, and provide human justice. Paul says these are God's servants to do us good, verse 4. They are not authorized to kill someone because they think they committed a crime. They are, however, authorized to use lethal force if a person is a danger to others, and refuses to surrender. The law, which takes into consideration a much wider assortment of facts than the moment a threatening situation appears can possibly do, should use greater discretion. When a person's life is being threatened, it is right for law enforcement to protect innocent life, even if that means that the perpetrator may end up losing theirs.

However, too often, law enforcement is used with a heavy hand. Race and prejudice often twist the judgement of those who have to make quick decisions.

In the courtroom, when all the facts are laid out, and there is no imminent danger to life, a different process can begin to take place, one that reaffirms the value of life, not one of bitterness and vengeance. Life at that point is to be preserved, while making sure the perpetrator will never have the opportunity to hurt another human being again.

We can all feel vindictive at times. We long for justice, and so many consider that the death penalty is a fair punishment if a person's life has been taken in an act of violence and cruelty. However, we must consider Jesus' words to the disciples in Luke 9:55, 56. James and John were willing to call fire from heaven to consume the Samaritans who did not receive Jesus. He rebuked them, saying: *"You do not know what manner of spirit you are of. For the Son of Man did not come to destroy men's lives but to save them."* NKJ.

Jesus immediately identified the spirit that James and John were being influenced by. It was not the Spirit of God which seeks to save those who are lost. It is the spirit of condemnation, division, hatred, and pride.

Only a little earlier in the very same chapter of Luke, James and John had witnessed God's amazing power and declaration of Fatherhood as they saw Jesus transfigured into an image of His eternal glory. How quickly the disciples allowed that amazing transformative experience turn into vindictive hate, and feeling of superiority!

Furthermore, we read in 2 Peter 3: 9 how the Lord is not slack concerning His promise, *"not willing that any should perish but that all should come to repentance."* NKJ. God does not want to send anyone to hell. He is not that kind of God. He loves us with an everlasting love.

He wants to heal us, to restore us to Himself.

God's gift to us is eternal salvation, Romans 6:23. If understanding God's grace towards us is somehow difficult for you, perhaps you have never asked God to forgive you for your sins. The Bible teaches that _all have sinned and fall short of the glory of God, and are justified freely by His grace_, Romans 3:23. NIV. If we think that our good lives and upright standing in society earn us God's favor, we are being deceived. The Bible is very clear that we all need to repent of our sins, and the only way we can ever enter God's presence is through the redemptive work of Christ.

Won't you ask Him now to forgive you your sins through the finished work of Christ on the cross? It is never too soon to do so. We do not know when God is going to call us into eternity. Then, it is too late to decide whose team we are on. We do not own our next breath. We do not know what happens tomorrow. Life is very short. So do it now. Today is the day of salvation.

Chapter Three: True Safety vs False

"Put away your sword," Jesus told him. "Those who use the sword will die by the sword."

Matthew 26:52 NLT

On the afternoon of Thursday, September 19, 2024, a shocking tragedy unfolded inside the Letcher County Courthouse in Whitesburg, Kentucky. District Judge Kevin Mullins was fatally shot by Letcher County Sheriff Mickey Stines, following a reported argument between the two. Judge Mullins suffered multiple gunshot wounds and was pronounced dead at the scene. Sheriff Stines was taken into custody and has reportedly cooperated with investigators, according to Trooper Matt Gayheart of the Kentucky State Police.

This incident should stir more than momentary disbelief—it demands deeper reflection. This was not a random act of violence in a troubled neighborhood; it was a fatal shooting within the very heart of our justice system. A sheriff—entrusted to uphold the law— turned his weapon on a judge, whose role is to interpret and deliver justice. What kind of dispute could possibly justify such a breakdown of civic duty and moral restraint? The ramifications of this act stretch far beyond one courtroom—they ripple out to the public, especially our youth, sending a dangerous message about conflict resolution and the misuse of authority. It challenges us to confront how we model justice, accountability, and respect for life in our society.

There are many arguments made that claim guns do not kill, but people do. There is a nugget of truth in that, for sure. However, guns kill people faster and more effectively than most other methods. The US gun homicide rate is 26 times higher than that of other high-income countries. If more guns in the hands of the public made us safer, America would be the safest country on earth. But as we can see, that is not the case. Guns in the home increase the risk that anyone in the house, including children, will die by firearm suicide or unintentional injuries. And domestic abusers with access to a gun are five times more likely to kill their female victims. This should give us pause when considering how to protect our families. Currently, 4.6 million children live in households with at least one loaded, unsecured gun. Even if you don't have a firearm in your own home, your children can become victims in one of these homes, where children and teens may have access to unsecured guns. Every year, hundreds of children aged 17 and under gain access to a loaded gun and unintentionally shoot themselves or someone else - sometimes fatally. Nearly one in three of these shooters are ages five and younger. Guns were the leading cause of death for children ages 1-19 in 2020 and 2021 in the United States. The second were vehicle-related injuries. This is crazy. Talk about preventable causes of death!

We people are evil by our very nature. You don't have to watch little toddlers playing together very long before you see two of them trying to fight over a toy or some other perceived benefit, such as a cookie, or a favorite seat. We are selfish and self-seeking by nature. No one had to teach us to be that way. We also like to think that we are right, while the other person is, of course not, should they disagree with our point-of-view. This is called original sin. It follows us from birth to our graves. Paul put it this way in Romans 7:19: *"For I do not do the good I want, but the evil I do not want is what I keep on doing."* ESV. It is almost like sin is instinctive to us humans. Just like the birds know where to fly to escape the rigors of winter weather in the warmer climes of the south, so our souls instinctively lead us to mischief, unless we train our minds and put on the mind of Christ. In Philippians 2:5 we read: *"Have this mind among yourselves, which is yours in Christ Jesus, who, though he was in the form of God, did not count equality with God a thing to be grasped, but emptied Himself, by taking the form of a servant, being born in the likeness of men. And being found in human form, He humbled Himself by becoming obedient to the point of death, even death on a cross."* ESV

So, how does this relate to our epidemic of gun violence? I believe that guns give their owner a sense of entitlement and power, which then clouds the judgement of the bearer should emotions run high. Why would a person ever purchase a gun unless they were planning to use it? I believe this is the crux of the problem with guns. Even though shooting and killing people is illegal, our laws allow an inordinate number of weapons to be roaming on our streets and neighborhoods. Guns provide an implicit approval, by society at large, to use them. When under emotional stress, we, therefore, resort to using them against our better judgment. The ground has been prepared; the seed has been planted. Now all we have to do wait for the right moment. This is where the deception lies. This is where all of satan's forces are empowered to war against whatsoever is pure, lovely, commendable, excellent, or worthy of praise. These are the things we are to think about, according to Philippians 4:8. When holding a gun in your hand, how do you accomplish that?

What about self-defense? Is it not my duty to protect myself? Jesus actually answered this question with words that even most non-believers can easily bring to mind: *"If someone strikes you on the right cheek, turn to him the other also,"* Matthew 5:38. NIV. This was Jesus teaching in the famous Sermon on the Mount. Why do we choose to ignore our Lord's clear admonition?

This is similar to the dichotomy we encounter with alcohol. There are rules and laws against drunk driving, or driving under the influence. Yet there are bars that are mostly accessible by cars only and whose clientele drive cars. So, it seems like there is a double standard. The laws are strict when it comes to drunk driving, yet society nods favorably in the direction of easy availability. As a result of this, about 32 percent of traffic crash fatalities in the United States involve drunk drivers. In fact, on average, over the 10-year period from 2013-2022, about 11,000 people lost their lives in drunk-driving crashes, according to the National Highway Traffic Safety Administration.

Just like open roadside bars extend an invitation for folks to just relax and have a few foamy ones "for the road," the same way guns lure people to set aside their reasoning to "make a point", to revenge, or just to let out their frustrations at the expense of others.

However, if we compare this statistic to gun deaths in the United States, one will discover we are encountering an even greater problem. In 2022, 48,204 people died from firearm incidents in the United States. In 2023, that number was 46,728, according to CDC. Every year, on average, 117,345 people are shot. In 2023, 46, 728 people died in the United States from gun related causes. On average, one person is killed by a gun every eleven minutes according to according to Johns Hopkins Bloomberg School of Public Health. Gun suicides accounted for 58 percent of these deaths, while 38 percent were homicides.

In comparison, in 2023, 12, 429 individuals were killed due to alcohol-impaired driving, according to the National Highway Traffic Safety Administration (NHTDA). While we have organizations, such as MADD, or Mothers Against Drunk Driving, trying to bring awareness to this serious and troublesome issue, we may question what we as believers are doing to reduce gun deaths, which represent over three times as much tragedy and loss?"

And yet, we are seemingly okay with the fact that in this country, we presently have more guns than people!

We have lost our respect for human life, and it shows in many, many ways in our society.

As believers, our ultimate hope must never rest in the systems or politics of this world. Yet, Jesus calls us to live with discernment— "wise as serpents and innocent as doves" (Matthew 10:16). This means we are not to be naïve or passive in the face of reality. We must be willing to acknowledge and engage with truth, especially when it is presented through credible sources. Our responsibility begins within: pursuing righteousness and truth in our personal lives. From there, we are called to extend that pursuit outward—into the spheres of influence God has entrusted to us, and ultimately, into the broader society. In doing so, we become faithful stewards of both wisdom and witness in a world desperately in need of both.

A gun in a home is about eight times more likely to be used against one of the occupants of the home than any intruder. And more often than not, if an intruder enters the home, the gun is going to be used against the person owning it, not the other way around.

Guns are also the most commonly used tool for suicide. In 2023, gun suicides in the United States reached an all-time high, with 27,300 people dying by firearm suicide. The annual rate of firearm suicides in 2023 is 8.16 per 100,000 people. In fact, over half of all gun related deaths are suicides. Gun suicide attempts are also more lethal compared to other methods, such as pills.

Children's access to guns is another issue that highlights the problems of considering guns being protective. Far too many children's lives have been cut short inadvertently as they find a gun their parents carelessly left in their reach. An item that was intended to protect the family has now become the source of the most grievous pain imaginable. Active shooter drills in schools do little to help our young ones deal with the trauma and tragedy of easily available firearms. Instead, they almost serve to make these indescribably cruel, violent, and most of all preventable events seem "normal," like a hurricane, or other natural disaster. A hurricane or tornado may not be easily preventable. A firearm mass murder, however, is.Guns are just about the only consumer products on the market that have the exclusive purpose of killing and maiming. In the hands of police, the military, and trained security personnel, they serve a vital function. In the hands of civilians, they often wreak havoc like few other manmade things can, apart from bombs or nuclear weapons, perhaps. Why do we make it so easy for anyone to obtain one in the face of the incredible violence that we face just about every day?

In September 2024, there have been 16 school shootings in the State of Georgia alone! Four people were recently gunned down at Apalachee High School. What are we teaching our children?

Violence? Vindictiveness? Revenge? It is time for believers to wake up.

As believers, our safety is not found in weapons. Paul stated it this way: *"For the weapons of our warfare are not carnal, but mighty through God for pulling down of strong holds,"* 2 Corinthians 10:4. KJV. Weapons kill, maim, and destroy lives, just like Jesus said in John 10:10. Weapons do not heal. They do not bring comfort or peace. They don't resolve anything. They are a tool the enemy uses to bring destruction on families, schools, work places, streets, lives, and society as a whole. In its wake it leaves broken homes, broken dreams, lives cut short, or maimed.

Our security is found in the Lord. Proverbs 18: 10 puts it this way: *"The name of the Lord is a strong tower; the righteous runneth into it, and is safe."* NKJ.

Also, in Psalm 118: 6, we read: *"The Lord is on my side; I will not fear: what can man do unto me?"* ESV.

Psalm 91 is one of the most poignant reminders to us of God's ever-present protection and care of His children. Read it and then reread it. You will not regret what you did.

Over and over again, we are told in the Bible to not fear. I have heard that there are 365 times in the Bible that we are told not to fear, one for each day of the year. I have not personally verified this number, but I know fear is talked about all over the Bible. The fear of God is the only fear we should embrace. Proverbs 9:10 states *"The fear of the Lord is the beginning of wisdom, and the knowledge of the Holy One is understanding."* NIV. Yet, as believers, we are just as likely to succumb to unreasonable fears as the world. Why is that? Is it because we do not want to put the Word of God into practice in our lives? We get diluted by the world. We watch the evening news and hear about another school shooting. It causes us to put our trust in metal detectors, active shooter drills, armed police, better gun laws, and so on. Those may be okay, but our true security is in doing God's will, step by step, day by day. Walking by faith requires that we go to the throne room of grace every day, lay down our burdens, and receive from our Heavenly Father what He wants us to have for each day. This gives us comfort in our trials, and reassurance that He has it all under His control. We do not need to fret because of evil doers, according to Psalm 37: 8. They shall be cut off.

As followers of Christ, we are called to turn away from anything that brings harm to life—whether it's substance abuse, unhealthy lifestyles, toxic relationships, environmental neglect, violent forms of entertainment, or weapons designed solely for destruction. These are not tools of righteousness—they are instruments of the enemy, crafted to kill, steal, and destroy. Why, then, would a believer ever embrace or harbor such things in their home? To do so stands in direct contradiction to the teachings of Jesus, who called us to be people of peace, love, and life-giving purpose. Our lives should reflect the values of the Kingdom, not the brokenness of the world.

The apostle Paul taught us about warfare against our enemy in Ephesians 6: 10-18. Our enemy is never individuals. Our enemy is the spiritual entity that presides over spiritual darkness in high places. This can take the form of a political power, or it can manifest itself in even the most minute details of life in the form of injustice, unfairness, greed, hypocrisy, violence, and so on. In other words, we are not to worry about evil people. Jesus put it this way in Matthew 10:28: *"And do not fear those who kill the body but cannot to kill the soul. But rather fear Him who is able to destroy both soul and body in hell."* NKJ. Who is He talking about here? God alone can determine issues of life and death. He is always just. His judgments are always fair. He does not miss a thing. He even counts the hairs on our head. Why would we not trust Him to do right for His people?

Evil people can connive against and destroy us physically, but if we submit to the One who holds ultimate power, and executes ultimate justice, we have nothing to fear. Jesus' words!

When we put death into eternal perspective, we should actually be praying for those who mistreat us or treated us with violence. Jesus commanded us to do so, too! He told us to love our enemies and pray for those who spitefully use and persecute us in Matthew 5: 44. But why would He tell us to do so?

I believe there are two reasons He told us to pray for our enemies.

Number one:

It will help us in our relationship with the Father, because He is the One who first forgave us for all of our transgressions against Him. We should do the same for those who have wronged us, just as Jesus taught us in His prayer.

Number two:

When we pray for our enemies, we invite God's transformative power into their lives—opening the door for His Spirit to stir their hearts toward repentance and eternal salvation. So why would we choose to kill those who seek to harm us, even if we have the legal right to defend ourselves? As believers, we already possess the assurance of salvation through the shed blood of Jesus Christ. But our enemies may not. If we were to take their lives, we may be cutting off their final chance to turn to God and receive His forgiveness. In contrast, if we were to lose our own lives in such a moment—while tragic—we would immediately enter the presence of our Heavenly Father, provided we have entrusted our lives to Christ. What greater hope could we hold than that? To choose eternal perspective over earthly reaction is to walk in the footsteps of Jesus Himself.

The question then to ask ourselves is this: Do I really believe what I profess with my lips, or is my faith as changeable as the leaves on an autumn tree? They first change their color, and then fall off.

My armor with God includes a shield of faith, according to Paul in the Ephesians passage we quoted earlier. How about the belt of truth? And don't forget the sword of the Spirit. The breastplate of righteousness. The helmet of salvation. The shoes of peace. Are we quick to make a wardrobe change when things get tough, or we simply aren't getting our way?

As Christians, it is our responsibility to expose facts that reveal the satanic efforts of our society to snuff out people's lives, whether through abortion, guns, the death penalty, drunk or impaired driving, easy access to illegal drugs, medical misinformation, contaminated soil resulting in compromised crops, chemical additives in our food supply, polluted air and water, or any other means. All people are created in the image of God. This is a unique privilege that mankind possesses. Animals were created by God also, but they do not bear the image of the Creator. We are the only ones that do. That is why it is our responsibility to protect life no matter what.

Chapter Four: Finding Truth in Chaos

"The king will reply, 'I tell you the truth, whatever you did for one of the least of these brothers of mine, you did for me.'"

Matthew 25:40. NIV

"There is a way that seem right to a man but in the end it leads to death."

Proverbs 14:12 NIV.

All life holds immeasurable value in the eyes of God, and He cares deeply for even the most overlooked among us. But who exactly are the "least of these" Jesus refers to? Could it be those society often ignores or pushes to the margins—those who differ from us in race, ethnicity, religion, social class, education, or political and economic viewpoints? Might He have been speaking of the disabled, the forgotten elderly, or the voiceless unborn—those most innocent, vulnerable, and tragically discarded? I believe He was speaking of all these and more. Jesus shattered human-made barriers, refusing to judge by appearance, status, or background. God sees us not through the lens of division, but through the lens of compassion. As Peter reminds us in 1 Peter 1:24, "All people are like grass," fleeting and fragile. Yet in stark contrast, the Word of the Lord endures forever (verse 25). And it is by that enduring Word that every life—especially the least among us—is given sacred worth.

So we have now established that all life is sacred, and worthy of our protection, whether in or out of the womb. God is not partial towards any person. In fact in 2 Chronicles 19: 7 advises us to judge carefully. *"For with the Lord our God there is no injustice or partiality or bribery."* NIV.

Jesus taught us in Matthew 7:1-2 to not judge other people. It says:

"Do not judge, or you too will be judged. For in the same way you judge others, you will be judged, and with the measure you use, it will be measured to you." NIV. Judging other people is always wrong. We are taught to love, and, at times, to correct others, if they are ready for that, and we have the opportunity to do so. It is not our place to judge others created in the image of God. However, we are to judge what is right and what is wrong in order not to fall into sin in our own lives. We can know how to judge certain actions based on the Word of God. Knowing God's Word provides us with a compass that leads us to make healthy and beneficial life choices.

God alone has the knowledge of all things. He alone is qualified to make judgments. Our job is to humbly follow what we have been taught in His Word, and teach others likewise.

Sometimes, we judge others without even realizing it. We may look at someone and determine in our hearts that we would never fall into such sin, that we would surely never give into such temptation as this poor soul did. This is called pride. James 4:6 states: *"God opposes the proud but gives grace to the humble."* NIV. It is amazing how, in today's culture, the word "pride" has been given new clothing, so to speak. Whether on the left or the right, people often talk about "pride" as a positive value, something one should aim for. It can be about pride for being an American, or pridefully displaying the American flag. Or, on the other hand, the pride of being "gay", or socially adjusted to accept deviations from God's original plan for mankind. While there is nothing wrong with loving our country, whether it be America, or another country, and there is certainly nothing wrong with loving people of all shapes, sizes, colors, or beliefs, we must not be foolish enough to consider pride to be a virtue to be promoted. Pride will often lead to hypocrisy. The word "hypocrisy" comes from the Greek word hypocrisies, which means "play acting". By being proud, are we actually play acting to be something we are not? Are we play acting this thing called "Christianity"? Are we truly ready to follow Jesus in all our actions, words, and thoughts? Or are we simply going through the motions to appear Christian because we believe Christianity is somehow better than other religions, philosophies, or thought systems? Jesus warned that not all who call Him 'Lord, Lord' will enter the kingdom heaven. But only those who do the will of the Father who is in heaven, Matthew 7:21.

Pride leads to feelings of superiority, the false sense that somehow we are better than other people. The Bible makes it very clear that God does not approve of pride as godly value. In James 4:6 we read

"God resists the proud. But gives grace to the humble." NKJV

In Proverbs 16:18 we are advised that pride goes before destruction, and a haughty spirit before a fall. As believers in Jesus, and followers of His teachings, we are to search our hearts for any remnants of the old adamic nature which seeks to satisfy selfish desires, including the tendency to want to be better than others. We are to replace that with a gracious attitude towards our fellow human beings. We have received grace as a free gift from our heavenly Father. We should therefore extend the same grace to others, without conditions, without pride, or a sense of superiority.

True faith requires action. It is about service to others, about putting others' needs ahead of our own. Paul writes in Philippians 2: 3-4 that we are to *"do nothing out of selfish ambition or vain conceit, but in humility consider others better than yourselves. Each of you should look not only to your own interests, but also to the interests of others."* NIV.

This is one of my personal favorite verses in the Bible. How I long to serve the Lord exactly in that way! But the world has a completely different agenda.

It is about achievement, gain, accomplishments, name, and fame.

The psalmist says in Psalm 119: 105 *"Your word is a lamp to my feet and a light for my path."* NIV.

We also read in the same Psalm verse 11: *"I have hidden your word in my heart that I might not sin against you."* NIV.

As we view each and every life as precious, the way God sees it, we begin to change our perspective on many aspects of our own lives. If God really loves me that much, and He loves other people just as much, then how am I to live my life having this knowledge?

Jude advices us, in Jude 20 to, *"But you, dear friends, build yourselves up on your most holy faith."* NIV. Jude is a short book towards the very end of the New Testament. Jude is believed to have been Jesus' half brother. What did he mean with our most holy faith? Can some faith be less holy? Absolutely. We can be sincere in our beliefs, and yet be totally misguided. Be can believe in Santa Claus as a real living, breathing person with extraordinary powers to meet the wishes of countless young children all over the world at the same time, for example. That is a form of faith we have often instilled in the very young. Yet, it is a false belief. In the same way, we can have false conceptions about the Bible, Jesus, the Christian faith. We may hold on to the false belief that Jesus was just another prophet; that His sacrificial death on the cross could not possibly atone for the sins of billions of people throughout history. Actually, that is a fairly common belief in today's culture. We may also believe that what Jesus taught us was indeed true, but that there are many other "prophets" who have had a similar message throughout history, and that there are many ways to God. Jesus is just one of those. Or we may believe that God has sent us a new prophet, such as Mohammed, for example, or Joseph Smith, who have the latest truth about how a person should be saved. But all of those are unbiblical substitutionary doctrines that we have been warned about repeatedly in the Scriptures. They may involve parts of the truth, but in their entirety, they are false and based on our own efforts to please God, not on the grace of God through the finished work of Christ. In Matthew 7:21 Jesus warns his disciples and those in His audience about false faith by saying, *"Not everyone who says to me 'Lord, Lord', will enter the kingdom of heaven, but only he who does the will of my Father who is in heaven."* NIV. So what is the will of the Father then? Let's read about it in John 6:40: *"For my Father's will is that everyone who looks to the Son and believes in Him shall have eternal life, and I will raise him up at the last day."* NIV.

Jesus then goes on to explain the kinds of things that people may mistakenly consider to be signs of true repentance and salvation. That includes some of the gifts of the Spirit, such a prophesy, or driving out demons. Those are powerful demonstrations of God's power, if indeed they are powered by the Holy Spirit. But we need to be careful not to attribute all miracles to God's Spirit. We need to be discerning of spirits. Jesus told us that there will be many who have held on to false beliefs in His name, and are in for a rude awakening when He comes to His own. His statement is: *"I never knew you. Away from me, you evildoers!"* Matthew 7:23. NIV.

We are also admonished by the apostle John to not believe every spirit, but to test the spirits to see whether they are from God, because many false prophets have gone out into the world. He then gives us the "litmus test" of true faith: *"This is how you can recognize the Spirit of God: Every spirit that acknowledges that Jesus Christ has come in the flesh is from God: but every spirit that does not acknowledge Jesus is not from God. This is the spirit of the antichrist, which you have heard is coming and even now is already in the world,"* 1 John 4: 2-3. NIV.

Jesus also gave us an easy, and reassuring way to remember the truth about salvation in His words to grieving Martha as her brother Lazarus had died while Jesus was still out of town: *"I am the resurrection and the life. He who believes in me will live, even though he dies; and whoever lives and believes in me will never die,"* John 11:25. NIV.

In John 3:16-18 we have the familiar dialog between Jesus and Nicodemus, who was a Pharisee and also a member of the Jewish ruling council. Jesus explained to Nicodemus first about the need to be "born again". This confused Nicodemus, as he was thinking about how a natural birth could possibly happen twice. Jesus explained to him that "flesh gives birth to flesh, but the Spirit gives birth to spirit," John 3: 6. This is a mystery. But as we recognize the work of the Holy Spirit, and are led by Him, we learn to lean on Him. Jesus then told Nicodemus about how God's love for the world caused Him to send His Son to the world to save the world, not to condemn the world. But salvation would depend on a person's acceptance of this free gift of God. *"Whoever believes in him is not condemned, but whoever does not believe is condemned already because he has not believed in the name of God's one and only Son,"* John 3:18. NIV.

We've established that having the right kind of faith is essential—but faith is anything but stagnant. It's not merely an intellectual agreement with something we cannot see. In fact, many of the things we accept as real are invisible to the naked eye. Have you ever seen oxygen? Gravity? Rising humidity? Or the thinning of the atmosphere at high elevations? We believe in them not because we've seen them directly, but because we observe their effects. We can't see oxygen molecules, yet we know how vital they are—and what happens in their absence. Gravity, too, remains unseen, yet its pull governs every step we take and every leaf that falls from a tree. Leaves never fall upward, unless caught in a powerful wind—another invisible force we know only by the movement it causes. In much the same way, faith may be invisible, but its presence is evident through the impact it has on our lives.

Faith is action. It is an active acknowledgement of God in every sphere of life. Faith that acknowledges the truths of the Bible but then does not act upon those truths is dead, James 2:26.

In Hebrews 11:1 we read that *"Faith is the substance of things hoped for, the evidence of things not seen.* KJV. There are challenges in life that we all face that put our faith to the test. We must be willing to grow in our faith, and build ourselves on those principles that we learn through obedience to God's Word. How do we handle divisive political and sociological chasms in today's world, for example? Or how do we interact with an unfair employer, coworker, an aggressive driver, or and unpleasant grocery clerk? This is where we need to follow the guidance of the Holy Spirit.

Biblical faith goes far beyond intellectual assent—it engages the heart, shapes our motives, influences our words, and directs our actions. True faith is never passive; it transforms us. If we genuinely believe that Jesus Christ is the Son of God, who came to die for our sins and rose again, then that belief should turn our entire lives upside down. Such faith isn't compartmentalized; it permeates every part of who we are—or at least, it should. This is the very challenge Jesus issued to the church in Laodicea in Revelation 3:16, when He warned that because they were lukewarm—neither hot nor cold—He would spit them out of His mouth. Lukewarm faith has no power to change lives. Real faith demands more.

The church of Laodicea may have heard the gospel and received it with joy in their hearts. They may have been excited, and had some tent meetings, seen the healing power of God, and heard amazing sermons from the apostles. They felt the power and majesty of the Father and yet something was missing in their hearts. If someone is cold towards the gospel, there is hope for them because they may not have been exposed to it fully as of yet. If they are on fire for the Lord, that is fantastic! That is what He wants. But if they are lukewarm, they have mostly likely worn out the pews of a church for many years without any visible signs of a life transformation. They may have the appearance of godliness, but lack the power thereof. They are not bearing fruit, as Jesus described in John 15: 5-6 as He was talking about the vine and its fruitful branches, and then the unfruitful branches, that did not produce fruit because they did not remain in the vine, which is a picture of Jesus. If we remain in Him, we will bear fruit in our lives that produces what Paul describes in Galatians 5:22-23 as the fruits of the spirit. These include love, joy, peace, patience, kindness, goodness, faithfulness, gentleness, and self-control. I believe it also includes a vibrant witness of the truth of salvation to others.

There are two primary ways we grow in faith and deepen our understanding of God's will. The first is through consistent engagement with His Word. This is why we're called to search the Scriptures daily—to absorb the truth, apply it, and allow it to shape our lives. The more we know, the more we grow—and the more we grow, the more we desire to know. This ongoing pursuit leads us into a clearer understanding of God's will and draws us into a closer walk with Jesus. When we face difficult choices or seek guidance in life's pivotal moments, we're meant to turn to the highest source of truth—the deep well of God's Word. It is there that we find wisdom, direction, and stability. This is what it means to build ourselves up in our most holy faith, as encouraged in Jude 1:20 (NKJV).

Building ourselves on our most holy faith means that when we are uncertain about a certain circumstance, about whether it is within God's will for us or not, we should always reach for the higher option, the one that leaves no question about being within the will of God.

This brings us to the second tool we are to use when seeking God's will: Jesus said that the Holy Spirit will lead us into all the truth, John 16: 13. So the easiest way to accomplish this is to seek Him daily, for matters great and small in our lives. The Holy Spirit is our guide. He will convict us of wrong motives, selfish actions, vain thoughts, and thoughtless words. Because He always seeks to glorify God, we can trust that He will not lead us down the wrong path. He also cares for us, and provides comfort, truth, rest, reassurance, and hope for us when we face trials and various temptations. He loves us, just as Jesus loves us. His intentions towards us are always good.

So, how do we get this relationship with the Holy Spirit? It is through prayer. Consistent, and persistent prayer. The Holy Spirit is never further from us than our next breath. If we call on Him to comfort us, love us, calm us down when we are overwhelmed with fear, loss, anxiety, or regret, He will be there for us. This is God's promise. In His farewell address Jesus promised that He would never leave us nor forsake us.

"And surely I am with you always, to the very end of the age,"

Matthew 28:20. NIV.

And in Hebrews 13: 5 we read: *"Never will I leave you; never will I forsake you"*. NIV. Could there be any more reassuring words for us to hold on to than these? If God so cares for us, and promises to be with us no matter what happens, that same promise is also extended to the entire human race, as long as we put our faith and trust in Him!

Chapter Five: Peace Over Conflict

"Who is it that overcomes the world? Only the one who believes that Jesus is the Son of God."

(NIV) 1 John 5:5

"For the weapons of our warfare are not carnal, but mighty in God for pulling down strong holds, casting down arguments and every high thing that exalts itself against the knowledge of God, bringing every thought into captivity to the obedience of Christ."

2 Corinthians 10: 4-5 NKJV.

"The Lord will fight for you; you need only to be still."

Exodus 14:14 NKJV.

"Blessed are the peacemakers, for they will be called sons of God."

Matthew 5:9. NIV.

In previous chapters, we've explored significant topics related to Christian ethics as revealed in the Holy Scriptures—issues such as the justice system, capital punishment, the role of firearms in society, spiritual warfare, and the foundational tenets of our faith. Yet there remain other pressing matters that fall under the broader theme of what some have called a "culture of death." How should we, as followers of Christ, respond to difficult and deeply emotional questions like euthanasia (or mercy killing), suicide, war, environmental responsibility, and animal cruelty? Among these, one of the most divisive and emotionally charged topics today is abortion. Since the overturning of Roe v. Wade by the Supreme Court on June 24, 2022, the debate has only intensified, as decisions surrounding abortion access now fall to individual states.

As a community of compassionate believers, how are we to engage with these complex, often polarizing issues? Are they addressed in Scripture, and if so, how should we interpret and apply biblical principles to them in today's world? We will explore abortion in greater detail a little later, but first, let's begin to unpack the broader moral and spiritual questions that challenge our culture— and our faith.

With rapidly developing medical advances, there are often questions about when should life-preserving measures be ended in cases of terminal illness. Is euthanasia ever condoned in the Bible?

Another issue that is often discussed in this context is military service, the taking of lives due to political associations, or for protection of one's own homeland.

These questions are complex and not easily addressed, even in a format like this. Let us try to untangle some of the misconceptions, gray areas, and myths related to these issues.

Since we believe that every life has value, from conception to natural death, we must be careful as Christians not to condone euthanasia, or assisted suicide as an option. Euthanasia means that a healthcare professional assists in administering the lethal dose of medication in order to end life, as requested by the patient. Assisted suicide involves a person doing the action themselves, either guided by a medical professional, or independently, in order to precipitate death in the face of either a terminal illness, or unbearable physical, or emotional pain. Terminal illness, of course, is often accompanied by unrelenting and extreme pain.

While intolerable pain is certainly something that should be addressed as best as possible by the medical community, ending a life prematurely is never God's best for His creation. God understands pain. He Himself suffered incredible pain for us on the cross. His heart is tender towards all who suffer, and He is an ever-present help in times of our deepest trouble. We understand that pain has a purpose in our lives too, just like laughter, joy, and fulfillment have a purpose. Pain tests and refines our faith, it builds humility and compassion towards those who are suffering also. It can also bring healing as we realize our own limitations, and learn to lean on our all-knowing, all powerful Heavenly Father.

In our hour of trial, whatever the cause, we can always turn to the Word of God. In Psalm 46: 1 we read: *"God is our refuge and strength, an ever-present help in trouble."* NIV In Jeremiah 30:17 we read this promise: *"But I will restore you to health and heal your wounds."* NIV. We know that God is able to heal by His power any and all diseases. Yet, He does not always heal us the way the pray. But even in our darkest hour, when all hope seems lost, He is still there, just as he was with the three young men who were cast into the fiery furnace in Daniel 3. If you are not familiar with this story, you may take a moment to read it. God's protection was on the three young men despite the most horrific punishment they were suffering due to their unwavering faith in God. No matter what trial you may be facing today, you have the promise of God to be with you through the trial.

The apostle Paul put it this way: Romans 8: 18 *"I consider that our present sufferings are not worth comparing with the glory that will be revealed in us."* NIV. Paul knew more about suffering than most of us ever will. He was shipwrecked, stoned and left for dead, falsely imprisoned several times, gossiped about, scourged, and despised. Yet his attitude was one of thankfulness, as we particularly see in the letter to the Philippians, which was written while he was in prison chained to his guards not knowing how much time he had left on this earth.

We can rest assured that suicide is not the deadly sin that would cause a person to miss out on heaven if he or she has confessed faith in the Savior. Once we are His, nothing can snatch us out of His loving hands, John 10: 28, 29. Paul said it this way: *"For I am convinced that neither death nor life, neither angels nor demons, neither the present nor the future, nor any powers, neither height nor depth, nor anything else in all creation, will be able to separate us from the love of God that is in Christ Jesus our Lord."* Romans 8: 38-39 NIV.

The enemy would be glad to get us discouraged, have us doubt our faith and our commitment to the Lord. But we know that God is faith building even when we lose our faith at times. He does not reject us because of one moment of weakness. However, we are to seek the Lord daily and put on the armor of God so we can be strong in following His will, and trusting Him with all our earthly needs.

Passive euthanasia may involve discontinuing prescribed treatment. This is also called palliative care, or, in some instances, hospice care. Hospice care is generally provided for individuals with a life expectancy of less than six months. Only care that enhances quality of life is given. Life is not artificially prolonged by seeking new treatments or therapies. Equipment, such as ventilators, IVs, or artificial nutrition, may be discontinued, or not considered. This is very different from actively seeking to end life. Many sincere Christians seem to believe that they should allow life to continue interminably through breathing tubes and artificial nutrition administered via various feeding tubes inserted in the stomach, or via parenteral nutrition, which is administered via intravenous access points, regardless of the prognosis of the patient. They feel it is their obligation to prolong the life of their loved ones for as long as possible under any and all circumstances, regardless of the prognosis, or quality of life.

While I believe decisions about life-prolonging treatments are deeply personal, it's important to recognize that many of these medical interventions are relatively new when viewed against the backdrop of human history. Their use should be approached with discernment—both because of the high financial cost and the uncertainty of their outcomes. In some cases, such treatments can be a blessing, offering meaningful extensions of life. In others, however, they may unintentionally hinder the peaceful transition that both the patient and their loved ones might ultimately desire. Each situation is unique and must be considered carefully. Choosing to forgo treatment does not mean one is anti-life. In fact, there are times when discontinuing aggressive medical care can result in a more comfortable and dignified final chapter, free from the side effects of medications and the complications of invasive procedures. For many, passing in the comfort of a familiar, homelike setting—surrounded by loved ones—offers a far more meaningful experience than the sterile sounds of monitors and the constant motion of a hospital ward.

As believers, we are called to seek the guidance of the Holy Spirit in these moments. Trusting Him to lead us in knowing when, or if, life-prolonging measures should be continued is both wise and faith building.

If you know someone who has made the decision to end their own life, you are certainly not alone. Suicide certainly leaves a void that may seem unbearably huge and difficult to cross. The pain it leaves behind is unique, as it may leave loved ones wondering what they perhaps should or could have done differently to avoid this outcome. Suicide among young people especially seems to have reached epidemic proportions. For many, life does not offer great promise as there is so much societal unrest and uncertainty. Personal losses, school bullying, financial difficulties, relationship issues, disappointments in professional accomplishments, as well as addictions, and legal problems, can all lead to hopelessness and despair. Young people can hardly look to the older generations to provide guidance in difficult situations, as they also seem, in many cases, equally lost. The pace of change in our society is disorienting. The rules that applied in previous generations no longer appear to have relevance today. Some young people find it difficult to obtain a college education due to the costs involved. And many who choose to pursue college degrees graduate with debts larger than a downpayment on a house. They may feel trapped. Or worse. Many choose to end their lives in hopes of making the pain of disappointments and failures go away. However, as believers in Christ and having the hope of eternal life, we know this life, no matter how hard things may seem, is not the final state. In fact, the apostle Paul said in Romans 8:18 that our present sufferings are not worth comparing with the glory that will be revealed in us. WOW! Paul had experienced suffering on a much larger scale than most of us can even imagine. James tells us in James 1: 2-4 to consider it "pure joy" whenever we face trials of many kinds. As difficult as it is to rejoice in sufferings, we can be assured that nothing happens to us without the Father's knowledge and approval. He knows us better than we know ourselves. He will also provide us with the strength to withstand whatever it is that we are facing as we put our full trust in Him. As Jesus' followers, we have the privilege of knowing that this life is not all there is. God has better things planned for us, and we can fully put our faith and trust in this truth.

If we encounter suicide in our family or among our loved ones, we must remember that Jesus died for all our sins, past, present, and future. As long as we put our faith in His work of redemption, nothing can separate us from the love of God, Romans 8: 38-39. Even death cannot separate us from the love of the Father. Not even death by suicide. There are no exceptions.

In God's Kingdom—what may seem upside down to the world but is, in truth, the only Kingdom truly right side up—suffering is transformed. It is not meaningless. Through Christ, we are reassured that the pain we endure on earth is temporary, and we are shown, by His own example, how to walk through suffering with grace. On the cross, Jesus endured it all—humiliation, physical agony, rejection, and betrayal—all at once. Even more, He experienced the aching sense of separation from God the Father, whom He loved with all His heart and whose will He had come to fulfill. Yet He did not protest. He did not curse His executioners. Instead, He prayer for the Father to forgive them. His heart remained tender, even toward those who inflicted such unimaginable pain.

This was not the end—it was the beginning of God's ultimate plan of redemption. Jesus wore the crown of suffering so that we could wear the crown of life. He carried the weight of the cross to open the door to eternal life for all who would follow Him.

Suffering also grows us in our walk with Christ here and now. We are not to look for suffering as something to be desired. However, we mature more when trials come, when things don't go quite the way we planned. Or when we encounter sickness, failed relationships, job loss, loneliness, or even persecution because of our faith.

But this hope of a new life with Christ in heaven does not excuse us from our duties on this earth. We must not become so heavenly minded that we are no earthly good, as the old saying goes. We are to occupy, to busy ourselves with God's business. And what is God's business, you might ask. Matthew 28: 19-20 sums it up this way:

"Go ye therefore, and make disciples of all the nations, baptizing them into the name of the Father and of the Son and of the Holy Spirit: teaching them to observe all things whatsoever I commanded you: and lo, I am with you always, even unto the end of the world." (ASV)

Our jobs on this earth are not done until we are called home.

But what about those who are doing military service for our country, you may ask. Is it biblical to pick up weapons of warfare against our national enemies? What if innocent civilians are killed as a result of our actions?

This is a question that is fairly complex. The Old Testament is full of battles fought and won, and some that were lost, as the Israelites took possession of the Promised Land. But the battles did not end there. The kings of Israel fought battles with surrounding nations hundreds of years later. King David was a warrior king. He became famous after slaying Goliath, the Philistine, at a young age with a smooth stone he picked up from a riverbed. After Goliath fell down on his face, David unceremoniously cut off his head with his own sword.

However, some of what David did in fighting these battles must have displeased the Lord as he was not allowed to build the temple of the Lord as he so wanted to do. He had gathered all the materials and was eager to start, but the Lord told him he could not. He had too much blood on his hands, as he himself admitted to his son Solomon in 1 Chronicles 22: 1-10. In 2 Peter 3:9 we read that God is not willing for any person to perish. In that context it is talking about eternal perishing, rather than death, but still. The truth is that much bloodshed not only leads to the death of many, but it also results in the eternal damnation of many souls on both sides of any conflict. That is why wars are not something to be glorified by a believer in Jesus, although there may be situations where wars are justified.

The Old Testament contains many accounts of violence and death, much of it unfolding in the context of war or divine judgment. At times, God directly disciplines His people for their rebellion, as seen in Numbers 21:4–9. When the Israelites grumbled against Moses about their journey through the wilderness and the food provided, their ingratitude led to a grave consequence—God sent venomous serpents among them, and many died. Yet even in judgment, God offered mercy. He instructed Moses to craft a bronze serpent and lift it high on a pole. Those who looked upon it in faith were healed.

This moment foreshadows the ultimate salvation found in Christ. Just as the bronze serpent was lifted up as a symbol of deliverance, so Jesus would be lifted up on the cross—becoming sin for us and offering healing from the fatal bite of sin. Through Him alone, we find life, restoration, and grace.

At other times, God would give the Israelites amazing victories over their enemies, such as is described in the book of Joshua when the city of Jericho was surrounded. The Israelites were told to circle the city daily for seven days, and on the seventh day, when they did that and blew the trumpets, the thick walls of the city crumbled down, Joshua 6.

In the book of Judges, chapter 7, we read about Gideon, who had an army of 32,000 men to fight against the Midianites and the Amalekites. In God's eyes, this was far too many. So He whittled the army down to 300. In the end, the enemy was so scared of the Israelites that they ended up attacking each other and running away. God was ultimately fighting the battle for them.

In the New Testament, we do not see descriptions of actual wars between nations, but we do see battles against spiritual forces. Paul writes in Ephesians 6: 12 that *"we do not wrestle against flesh and blood, but against the rulers, against the authorities, against the cosmic powers over this present darkness, against the spiritual forces of evil in the heavenly places."* ESV

Paul paints a vivid picture of how we're to face the unseen spiritual battles around us—not with physical weapons, but with a divine arsenal. Drawing from familiar images of warfare, he describes believers as being girded with truth, protected by the breastplate of righteousness, and grounded with the readiness that comes from the gospel of peace. He urges us to take up the shield of faith to extinguish the fiery attacks of the enemy, to wear the helmet of salvation, and to wield the sword of the Spirit—which is the Word of God. Notably, this sword is the only offensive weapon in the entire list; every other piece of armor serves to defend and protect the believer from spiritual harm. This powerful passage from Ephesians 6:11–17 lays the foundation for how we are to stand firm. But Paul doesn't stop there—he emphasizes what may be our most powerful weapon of all: persistent, Spirit-led prayer. He calls us to pray at all times, with alertness, perseverance, and intercession—not just for ourselves, but for all the saints.

In our world today, and especially in the United States, there is a strong belief that war, almost any war really, can be easily justified based on Old Testament scriptures. God is seen as a warrior God who chooses a side to fight on. If America stands for righteousness, then God will fight our wars for us. In the Old Testament, that is almost always Israel, unless they have sinned, in which case they may be defeated by their enemies. Defeat is the sign that the people of Israel have sinned and need to return to God. But in general, God fights on behalf of His people and scatters their enemies. We see this principle over and over again.

In Zechariah 4:6 we read *"Not by might, nor by power, but by My Spirit, says the Lord of armies."*

God can, and will, complete His intentions, either with or without our human weapons and armies. We read a remarkable story regarding the protection of the angel armies in 2 Kings 6: 8-23 against the army of a Syrian king. Elisha prayed that his servant's eyes be opened so that he could see the mighty army with horses and chariots of fire surrounding them for protection. And so God answered the prayer of Elisha, and his servant's eyes were opened. He could now see the invisible armies of heaven dispatched specifically for their protection. God is ultimately the force that directs nations' destinies. Turning to Him for protection in faith and truth delivers safety and security for all those who seek Him. And even in death a Christ-follower will not be shaken as they know that death does not hold the ultimate power over them. Jesus told us this clearly in Matthew 10:28 when He said: *"And do not fear those who kill the body but are not able to kill the soul. But rather fear Him who is able to destroy both body and soul in hell."* This was a reference to the eternal judgement of God over sin.

Truthfully, although the belief in the justification of military action has served us in some contexts, such as defeating the fascist tyranny of Nazi Germany, there have been several other instances where the bloodshed has not accomplished what it was intended for. Innocent lives have been slaughtered for little or no benefit, and the men and women in uniform have lost their lives, or limbs, on both sides. Justice was not served, although our men and women in uniform paid the ultimate price. Some return from the war scene disillusioned with life itself and commit hideous acts, and some end up killing themselves, as killing is now ingrained in their minds due to trauma they have suffered, as an option for consideration, as a model for behavior that at least in some instances is acceptable by society.

So, as people who believe in the sanctity of life, how are we supposed to deal with conflict between nations? Jesus was very clear in teaching us to pray for our enemies, Matthew 5: 43-48. And He told us that blessed are the peacemakers, for they will be called children of God, Matthew 5:9. He told us to turn the other cheek when confronted with brutality and injustice, Matthew 5:39. Some teach that this only applies to our personal enemies. I do not find that in my Bible. All people have been created in the image of God. Not all are children of God, however. The apostle John writes in 1 John 1: 12 that to all who did receive Him (Jesus), He gave the right to become children of God. So, to be clear, just because we are all part of God's creation does not automatically make us children of God. We must receive Jesus Christ as our Lord and Savior in order to be able to call God our Father.

As beings made in the image of God, as affirmed in Genesis 1:27, every person carries something sacred—an inherent worth that is both unique and god-like. Recognizing this divine imprint in others is not optional; it's essential. We are called to honor it, protect it, and treat it with the utmost care. This understanding should shape how we approach even the weightiest decisions—especially matters of war. Before declaring any military action as justified or unjustified, we must be willing to examine every angle: the motives, the objectives, the underlying forces. Is the action driven by genuine concern for the oppressed, or by national self-interest and financial gain? Does it serve to liberate and protect, or to conquer and exploit? These are not easy questions—but they're necessary ones if we truly believe in the value of every human life.

These are questions for the decision makers to decide. As individuals, we have little power to determine which conflicts are worthy of our military intervention as a nation. However, we do possess the ability to evaluate every situation, and measure it against the revealed Word of God. We can then decide whether or not this action earns our support or not. God does not task us to make decisions that have no implications for us personally. However, as much as it is in our power to work righteousness on the earth, that is our calling. Just like a skillful surgeon must cut through intact skin and flesh to get to where the cancer cells are hiding, so too, the military may have to strategically remove evil that could cause death and destruction. Nobody faults the doctor for what they are doing as being wrong, although this may cause pain and a difficult recovery for the patient. In the same way, there may be situations where military action is absolutely justified.

The thing to remember is that God does not favor one nation over another. Yes, He loves Israel, which is His special possession. Deuteronomy 7: 6 reads: *"For you are a people holy to the Lord your God. The Lord your God has chosen you out of all the peoples on the face of the earth to be His people, His treasured possession."* NIV. But even with Israel, He is strict and expects the Israelites to live lives that are worthy of their calling. No other nation has a special privileged position with God. As we have seen previously, God loved the whole world and gave up His Son so that whosoever believes in Him, can be saved, John 3:16. There are no limits to His love and care. There are no national barriers.

War, as a way to show military might or superiority in front of the world, will only lead to further conflicts. How can we honestly follow Jesus' command in Matthew 28 to go and make disciples of all nations, baptizing them in the name of the Father, and of the Son, and of the Holy Spirit, and teaching them to obey everything I have commanded you. And then go and blow them up in military action! This does not make any sense! We are either for God's Kingdom, or we are against it. Jesus said: *"He who is not with me is against me, he who does not gather with me scatters,"* Matthew 12:30. NIV. There is no middle ground. We don't want to be those who scatter, or destroy what God is doing in people's lives. We are to build up His church, the Kingdom. But each person has to seek the truth in their own heart. These are not words of condemnation. They are words to make us consider all sides of this issue.

SINIKKA PEMBER-COULTER

Chapter Six: Choose Life, Choose Health

"Before I formed you in the womb I knew you."

Jeremiah 1: 5.NIV.

"Now choose life, so that you and your children may live,"

Deuteronomy 30:19 NIV.

"You shall not murder,"

Exodus 20:13 NIV.

"Jesus said,' Let the little children come to me, and do not hinder them, for the kingdom of heaven belongs to such as these.'"

Matthew 19: 14 NIV.

"Children are a gift from the Lord; they are a reward from Him."

Psalm 127: 3 NLT

One of the most controversial and highly debated topics in today's world is the matter of abortion. Since Roe vs Wade was overturned by the Supreme Court on June 24, 2022, media outlets have been inundated with talking points on this issue. It appears most of the comments have been in favor of Roe vs Wade as it guaranteed access to abortion in the entire country. This appeared to many as a sign that abortion access would soon be eliminated or at least greatly restricted in much of the country. And this has been proven to be largely true.

According to the CDC (Centers for Disease Control), there were an estimated 613,383 abortions in 2022. This represents a two percent decrease from 2021. Approximately 93 percent of abortions occurred at 13 weeks of gestation or earlier. Early medication abortion (up to 9 weeks) accounted for 53 percent of all abortions.

Even though the overall abortion rate has been declining since 2008, according to CDC statistics, these numbers can be staggering to think about, and the societal impact is also severe as our population is aging, and fewer babies are born.

There is much we could discuss based on these numbers, but ultimately, our conversation here is not about the statistical data, or which ethnic groups are most affected by abortion, which states have the highest numbers, what are the economic impacts to take into consideration, or how we are going to provide social security benefits for our children's and grandchildren's generations. Instead, we will focus on the believer's perspective, and how we are to approach this very vital and central issue in our society today.

Certainly, raising a child that was not planned can be expensive in more ways than just financially. Raising a child is one of the hardest jobs in the world, and it is often not recognized as such. Mothers or fathers who choose to stay at home to raise their children are not compensated for their efforts in any way by society. Their work remains invisible to most.

The concept of family planning is often presented as a guaranteed path to control and certainty—but in reality, it's more myth than method, especially as promoted by the pro-abortion industry. In a perfect world, couples would choose exactly when to have children, how many to have, and move forward without fear of complications—no birth defects, no financial setbacks, no illness, no heartbreak. But life doesn't follow our scripts. Plans can crumble in the face of unexpected realities: infertility, miscarriage, job loss, or a pregnancy that arrives at an inconvenient time. While there's nothing inherently wrong with planning for a family, it must be done with humility and openness. Life is unpredictable. So, the real question becomes: what do we do when things don't go according to plan?

Instead of family planning, we should consider the fact all our steps are ordered by the Lord, Psalm 37: 23. In other words, as we seek to do His will in all matters, as we seek His righteousness, He will direct us better than we can because He knows us better than we know ourselves. We may face difficulties in life - everyone does- and Jesus even told us than in this world we would have troubles, John 16:33. He said: *"I have told you these things, so that in me you may have peace. In this world you will have trouble. But take heart! I have overcome the world."* (NIV)

As believers in Christ, we know that our lives are not our own. Our bodies are a temple of the Holy Spirit, according to 1 Corinthians 6: 19-20. Our call is to live holy lives in the midst of the chaos and unrest that surrounds us in the world. While we are not immune to troubles in the world, we are not to allow those troubles to control us. We should always direct our actions to bring about life, not death.

We also know that God's love is boundless towards those who confess their error. There is no sin that is beyond God's forgiving power. *"If we confess our sins, He is faithful and just to forgive us our sins, and to cleanse us from all unrighteousness,"* 1 John 1:9. NKJV. Abortion is not a "deadly sin" any more than any other sin we commit and ask for forgiveness for. The only sin that cannot be forgiven, is when we reject the gift of righteousness provided by the blood of Christ. That means that we have rejected His sacrifice because we trust ourselves to be good enough for God to accept us. I am sorry to break the news to you, but this will not lead you to eternal life. None of us are good enough on our own. Not a single one. We all have fallen short of God's standard. In Romans 3:23 the Apostle Paul writes: *"For all have sinned and fall short of the glory of God."* NIV. Newsflash: That includes you and me.

It can be hard for us to fully grasp that our actions may carry life-or-death consequences. In a world where the media often turns killing into entertainment, we've become desensitized. Movies glorify heroes who eliminate the "bad guys," and we cheer—not just for justice, but for the sense of resolution that follows. Deep down, we long for a righteous ending—for good to triumph over evil, for corruption, greed, and injustice to be defeated. We're wired to crave justice. But we're also conditioned to accept violence as the means to achieve it. We idolize the superheroes who descend from the sky, fists clenched, ready to destroy the enemy and restore order. We celebrate their victories, often overlooking the deeper question: Is violence the only path to justice—or just the one we've grown most comfortable with?

It is hard to imagine any other source for this type of heroic battle of good over evil, and good overcoming evil other than the Bible. Jesus is often seen as the "superhero" who comes and pulls us from the clutches of the evil serpent who lied to us and made us follow his ruinous path to our eternal destruction. But for Jesus… we would all be condemned to hell. And this is actually the gospel. This is what we know to be true. So, where is the discrepancy here?

When we take a closer look at the Jesus of the Bible, and compare His victory over sin and death with the typical superhero of

Hollywood or Disney, we see a completely different approach to overcoming evil. Jesus' approach was to give up His life voluntarily rather than fight evil using the methods and weapons of evil. Abraham Lincoln put it this way: "Do I not destroy my enemies when I make them my friends?"

Jesus prayed for those who put Him on the cross, because His kingdom was not of this world, John 19:11. He did not seek to be crowned with glory and honor in this life. Instead, He wore the crown of thorns, which were the result of our sin in the first place, according to Genesis 3: 17-19. They were part of the curse mankind took upon itself when we rejected God's simple command. Jesus wore the crown that resulted from our sinful decisions, both literally and symbolically! Christ knew that His Kingdom is an eternal Kingdom. He made Himself *"of no reputation, and took upon Him the form of a servant, and was made in the likeness of men,"* Philippians 2:7. KJV. Jesus, who was, in essence, God Himself, lowered Himself to be the servant leader of all of us so that He could save us from the effects of our sinful choices. Not only that, but He sacrificed Himself for us on the cross. He did not consider His own high standing when faced with the choice of saving us from ourselves. He did this willingly out of love for each and every person He created! What an amazing Savior we have!

The world's value system consists of putting one's own needs and comfort before anything else. The world teaches us to seek riches and fame to secure our future and to create a name for ourselves. Not all of that is bad or sinful. We are to take care of our families, and it is good to lead responsible, and productive lives. In Philippians 2: 4 Paul tells the Philippians to not look to their own interests, but each of you to the interests of others. In other words, we should care for the needs of our brothers and sisters in equal measure to how we care for our own needs. This is the path that Jesus showed us by His humility, grace, and care for others.

So, how are we to address issues like abortion in our world today? Does any of this have any relevance to the issue of abortion? The answer is: absolutely!

Abortion ends a life—one created by God—by cutting it apart while still in the womb and discarding it as medical waste, often labeled clinically as "products of conception." But beneath the language, we know the truth: this is human life. If we truly believed that a fetus was something less—that it lacked human DNA or the blueprint for personhood—we wouldn't feel the need to justify its destruction. It wouldn't threaten us. But we do know. We know that within that tiny body is the potential for skin, hair, a beating heart, and every feature that makes a human complete. And perhaps that's where the fear comes in—not of the science, but of the cost. Will this life take something from me? How will I provide for another child? What will this mean for my career, my relationships, my dreams? These questions are real—and they're heavy—but they also point to the undeniable truth that this life matters. Because if it didn't, we wouldn't wrestle with it so deeply.

These are real questions. They are not trivial. Life is demanding. It presents needs that are expected, and many more that are not expected. There are sicknesses, birth defects, congenital abnormalities, complications, undesirable personality traits, financial obligations, time constraints, family situations, and so much more. Life is complicated. As our understanding and knowledge has increased, so have the choices, decisions, and options that we all face on a daily basis. Knowledge does not always provide us with comfort and ease. Many times, the opposite is true. Knowledge and choices often fill us with anxiety and fear. Is what I am eating going to give me cancer, for example? Is the water I drink clean enough, or should I buy bottled water? What about the chemicals in plastic? All the phthalates, BPA, and such? What about fluoride? Is it good or bad? How about should I put my child in a public school, where he will learn the basics of reading, writing, and arithmetic, but where his soul may be left wanting for answers regarding life's deeper mysteries. Or should I provide him with a Christian education, which may give him a better understanding of the "big picture" of life, but may leave him unable to relate other youngsters who do not have this privilege? Will my child develop into a spiritual "snob" because of the choices I made for him?

Or will he model himself after what he sees happening in the public schools and at his friends' homes?

Should I vaccinate my children, as doctors routinely recommend, or should I pause and consider the scientific data that raises serious concerns—data that points to rare but often devastating side effects, chronic conditions, and, in some cases, even death? While these outcomes may not affect every child, the possibility is enough to stir deep uncertainty. Am I simply fortunate if my child escapes such complications? It's hard to know where the truth lies. Are any vaccines truly safe? At what point do the benefits outweigh the risks? And who can I trust to give me honest, unbiased information? Is this about protecting public health—or am I being swept into a system designed more for profit than well-being? If I refuse certain vaccines, will my child be barred from public school, missing out on friendships, learning experiences, and a sense of belonging? Could my well-intended caution unintentionally isolate him? Or worse—am I risking his health in ways I can't foresee? These are not easy questions. They deserve careful thought, compassion, and a deep sense of responsibility—for our children, and for the world we're raising them in.

As believers, we should always seek the Holy Spirit to guide us. He is the One whom Jesus called the Spirit of Truth in John 14:17. Jesus also said that the world cannot receive Him because it neither sees Him, nor knows Him. In Jesus' words, the world is not really even capable of discerning the truth that is contained in the Bible. It is as if it was written in a different language altogether.

When considering abortion, or any other life altering decision, we need to turn to the Word of God first. Is this issue addressed in the Bible, and if it is, how do I apply it to my current circumstances? In the cases of abortion, murder, guns, or the death penalty, we read that we are told not to kill. That is one of the ten commandments God gave to Moses on Mount Sinai as he was leading the Israelites out of Egypt and towards the Promised Land. It is pretty clear, therefore, that killing life is not what God would have us do. We find safety in the Word of God.

Secondly, we find courage to face difficulties and uncertainties by seeking the guidance of the Holy Spirit. He is always ready to guide us if we listen to His still small voice. We read about this in 1 Kings 19:12 when the prophet Elijah hears God's voice, not as loud cry or powerful experience, but as a small voice whispering in his ear. This is often how the Holy Spirit still speaks to us today. We just have to have ears to hear His voice.

In Proverbs 18:10 we read: *"The name of the Lord is a strong tower; the righteous run to it and are safe."* NIV. As mentioned before, one of the most comforting psalms regarding safety is Psalm 91. It addresses the major concerns we may still be facing today. Having come out of a worldwide "pandemic" just a few years ago, we learned how quickly the world can be turned into a state of absolute panic. Information, both real, and fabricated, quickly filled the internet. No one really knew who or what to believe, and the authorities convinced us to take drastic actions, which we may have willingly or reluctantly agreed to, just in case. It was hard to have loved ones isolated in hospitals and nursing facilities with no contact with even their closest family members. In many cases, there was no opportunity to bid farewell to a loved one surrounded by an army of health care workers covered from head to toe with isolation gowns, masks, face shields, and the like. Humanity was lost in favor of the scientific understanding of the moment.

Yet Psalm 91 tells us that we don't have to worry about these types of pestilences. Many Christians forgot to read their Bible, and read the newspapers or internet news sources instead.

This is not to say that we should ignore all public health information and just do our own thing with no regard for anything happening around us. What it does mean, though, is that we don't have to believe in and consent to every concept that is being spoon-fed to us as the absolute truth. We need to research information just like the Bereans did in Acts 17: 10-11. They were believers who wanted to make sure that what they heard from the apostles actually lined up with the Scriptures. It is not wrong to ask questions, or do research on your own. All of that is helpful and useful in weeding out false teachings, whether they be teachings of the Bible, or secular topics.

For example, we now know what we suspected all along but were not allowed to acknowledge, which is that the Covid 19 virus had its origins in a lab in Wuhan, China, and not in the wet markets where animals had been traded for hundreds or even thousands of years, as we were told by the "scientific community" at the time. We were told this story to cover up our own government's role in creating this monster. We now know the truth. And it is not pretty.

We must be circumspect and study things thoroughly. I think we have to be cautious when new information is piled on us as the "truth," and everything outside of that is labeled "misinformation." But in all things, we must acknowledge the presence of the Holy Spirit, who will always lead us to the truth. This was Jesus' promise in John 16: 13. He did not say that the Holy Spirit will lead us into some truth, or partial truth. He actually stated that the Holy Spirit will lead us into ALL truth! WOW! That is almost more than we can take in, isn't it? That God would give us this privilege, this Third Person of the Trinity, just so that we can learn how to walk out the gospel on this earth, here and now! This knowledge does not make us perfect, but it certainly makes us very blessed!

Chapter Seven: The Restoration of All Things

"The land produced vegetation: plants bearing seed according to their kinds and trees bearing fruit with seed in it according to their kinds. And God saw that it was good."

Genesis 1:12 NIV.

"'Love the Lord your God with all your heart and with all your soul and with all your mind.' This is the first, and greatest commandment. And the second is like it: 'Love your neighbor as yourself.' All the Law and the Prophets hang on these two commandments."

Matthew 22: 37- NIV.

"In everything, do to others what you would have them do to you,"

Matthew 7: 12. NIV.

"They will neither harm nor destroy on all my holy mountain, for the earth will be full of the knowledge of the Lord as the waters cover the sea."

Isaiah 11: 9.NIV.

In the previous chapters, we explored key themes related to the biblical view of human life and its inherent value. But to fully grasp our place in creation, we must also consider the broader context of life on Earth—and our God-given role within it. According to Genesis 1:26–28, humanity was entrusted with dominion over all living creatures. This responsibility was not one of domination, but of stewardship.

Genesis 2:15 further emphasizes this, describing how God placed man in the Garden of Eden to "work it and take care of it." Remarkably, the animals we were called to care for were created before us, underscoring the importance of our role as caretakers, not just inhabitants.

Another intriguing detail from Genesis 1:29 is that both humans and animals were originally plant-eaters. It wasn't until the fall in Genesis 3 that everything changed. When Adam and Eve succumbed to Satan's deception—choosing to believe a lie over God's clear instruction—the consequences were immediate and far-reaching. God had made His command simple and direct: they could eat from every tree in the garden, except the tree of the knowledge of good and evil. Disobedience would bring death (Genesis 2:16–17).

This foundational story reveals not only the weight of human responsibility but also the tragedy of turning from truth—and the deep grace of a God who still invites us into relationship, even after the fall.

Even today, we are faced with this same temptation to listen to other voices, rather than God's. We are bombarded with information daily via television, the internet, and social media sites. Some of it is true, but much of it is not. We can easily be led astray by what we read, as we discussed in an earlier chapter. The word of God is always our safety. Jesus said it Himself: *"Heaven and earth will pass away, but my words will never pass away,"* Matthew 24: 35. NIV. We can trust the One who is the "author and finisher of our faith," according to Hebrews 12: 2.

God's original plan was to preserve life, all life, and no animals would have been killed for food, clothing, or sacrifices. Yet all that changed as sin entered paradise. God Himself killed the first animal in order to make garments of skin for Adam and Eve in Genesis 3: 21. This was the first time blood was shed to cover up our sinful nature. The fig leaves that Adam and Eve had sewn together to cover themselves were entirely inadequate.

The Old Testament law, or Torah, which consists of the five books of Moses, the first five books of the Old Testament, is replete with animal sacrifices, starting in the book of Leviticus where the roles of the priests, the structure of the tabernacle, and the detailed descriptions of the animal and grain offerings, as well as the drink offerings are given. Yet none of those sacrifices could truly cover our sins. They were a temporary place marker to make us aware of the seriousness of sin and its consequences. The only sacrifice that could truly save us from sin was the blood that Jesus shed on the cross for all of us, for all time. We can read about this in Hebrews 10: 11-18. In verse 14 it states that *"by one sacrifice he (Jesus) has made perfect forever those who are being made holy."* NIV. And those who are being made holy are us, the ones who believe and follow Jesus. We are not holy in and of ourselves. Our righteousness is a gift from God.

The apostle John writes in 1 John 4:10: *"This is love: not that we loved God, but that He loved us and sent His Son as an atoning sacrifice for our sins."* NIV.

When we look ahead to what God has prepared for us, we catch glimpses of it in the book of Revelation—the final chapters of Scripture. In Revelation 11, the twenty-four elders worship God and speak of the coming judgments on the earth. And in a striking final phrase, they mention God's judgment on those who "destroy the earth." Have you ever considered that God might care deeply about how we treat the environment? That He, in fact, expects us to steward His creation wisely? We see this not only at the Bible's end, but also at its beginning. In Genesis, God entrusted humanity with the responsibility to care for the earth. As His image-bearers, we are meant to reflect His heart and His vision to the world around us— nurturing the land, protecting the creatures, and keeping creation pure. But if we're honest, can we say we've lived up to that calling? As a global community, have we truly honored the earth the way its Creator intended?

I would dare to say no. There are people who do care for the earth, believe in natural agriculture, animal welfare, and living a life that does minimal harm to the environment. Unfortunately, the majority of these brave souls are not professing Christians. This should not be so. Believers should be at the forefront of environmental justice, not sitting back and allowing our environment to self-destruct, with the false understanding that since God will create new heavens and a new earth, we have no obligation to care for the present one. God cares about His creation, and wants us to do the same.

In Isaiah 55, we see some beautiful imagery regarding the good things God will accomplish in the natural world upon the return of the exiles from captivity. This picture can be applied to the larger history of humanity as we are all exiled from paradise, and the only way we can ever experience the restoration of all things is through the redemptive work of Christ. In verses 10-11, God speaks of the natural order of rain and snow coming down from heaven, watering it and making it flourish.

God's promise to His people is expressed in verses 12-13: *"You will go out in joy and be led forth in peace, the mountains and hills will burst into song before you, and all the trees of the field will clap their hands. Instead of the thorn brush will grow the pine tree, and instead of briers, the myrtle will grow."* NIV.

We understand that much of this is poetic, but even so, it paints a picture of joy that we can all relate to. There is music and rhythm, and unspeakable joy that follows from the peace that only God can truly provide. And this peace is reflected in the very natural environment that God created.

In recent years we have seen this natural order broken more than possibly ever before. We've seen destructive floods in the south and the midwest, extreme drought conditions, especially in the west causing hundreds of fires destroying entire communities, not to mention forest land. We have seen land slides in burn scar areas, adding insult to injury. We have also seen the destructive power of tornadoes and hurricanes through much of the southern and eastern parts of the country. Climate patterns have been disrupted, and the seasons are changing, with extreme weather events becoming more common. The polar caps are melting at alarming rates, causing sea levels to rise, disrupting sea life, and annihilating animals that depend on the ice floes for survival.

Much of these changes are due to human activities, whether we want to admit it or not. We have micro plastics in our oceans, which are now found in most of our bodies as well. Carelessness regarding the environment is causing diseases and threatening our food supplies as well. As believers, we are to be good stewards of all the resources God has gifted us with.

We have created factory farms to produce our food, but in the process, we are abusing animals by overcrowding and poor diets that cause quick profits, but do not allow normal life spans or health for the animals, and we then overuse antibiotics to try to lessen the effects of these horrific living conditions. These antibiotics affect us too, and, in turn, create germs that become antibiotic resistant. This increases new infectious diseases that the pharmaceutical companies then try to find cures or vaccines for. It is a vicious cycle that is profit driven and has little to do with finding real solutions. In the end, by looking for shortcuts in food production, we are making ourselves sicker. As believers, we need to expose these unrighteous agricultural methods. We can make a difference in the health of our planet as well as the health of the souls of men.

So, where do we begin? Most of us don't hold positions of power that can shape national policy—but that doesn't mean we're powerless. If you are in a place to influence broader change, by all means, use it. But for the rest of us, real impact starts with personal responsibility. We can shift our consumer habits, become more mindful of how we use resources at home, and rethink the way we manage waste. Composting food scraps, recycling what we can, and choosing products with sustainable packaging are simple but powerful steps. I still find truth in that old phrase: *reduce, reuse, recycle.* It's short, but it says everything we need to hear. The United States, despite making up only four percent of the world's population, produces twelve percent of global municipal solid waste—more than China and India combined. We consume the most, recycle less, and waste more. This isn't about politics; it's about stewardship. God has entrusted us with His creation, and one day, we'll have to give an account. It's time we started living like that matters.

To be pro-life means that we are committed to the welfare of every person regardless of their age, gender, ethnicity, race, nationality, religion, or political affiliation. We do not have to agree with people in order to stand for their rights, or to seek their good. We also have to be able to look at the bigger picture, which includes all of God's creation. We are deeply intertwined with the physical world we are living in. We all know that if we were to ignore cleaning our homes for a period of time, refusing to take out the trash, washing the dishes, or doing the laundry, our homes would soon become unhealthy and eventually uninhabitable. How can we assume that we can continue to carelessly throw our trash on the streets, pile it in landfills, release it into the oceans, and beaches, and expect to live healthy lives?

A pregnant woman facing the weight of health care and day care expenses may see abortion as her only option. As believers, our responsibility goes beyond words—we are called to actively work toward a society where every person, regardless of employment status, has access to affordable health care.

Every human life is valuable—both the mother and her unborn child—and we are to reflect that truth through our actions. Justice, compassion, and love should guide our pursuit of a fairer society. It's not enough to offer sympathy or surface-level solutions. We must strive for lasting change—building systems that genuinely support women and families, especially those struggling to get by.

This is what Christ calls us to: not just to speak of grace, but to live it out by making family life not only possible, but dignified and supported.

In Isaiah 11 we see a beautiful description of the earth as it was originally intended to be, and how it will be again when Christ comes to rule it during the thousand-year kingdom. This will happen after the time of tribulation is completed, as described graphically in Revelation chapters 6 through 18. This period is rather brief, seven years, to be exact, but it will contain more horror and destruction than the earth has ever seen. It will be followed by a thousand years of peace and prosperity as satan and his minions are bound up, until the very end. The earth will flourish with beauty and splendor with Christ's rule. The animals will no longer seek to devour each other, as we see in Isaiah 11:6, and also in Isaiah 65: 25. The earth will be restored to its original design.

Chapter Eight: Invitation

"And we know that all things work together for good to those who love God, to those who are the called according to His purpose,"

Romans 8:28 NKJV.

I would like to stop here and revisit the scene I painted for you from my childhood at the beginning of this work. I was a child, feeling helpless, loved, but not fully understood. To me, the world seemed so unjust, so cold, so heartless. Even after I finally was released home from my two week's detention at the children's hospital, I would often tell my mother how bad the world was, and how someone needed to help this little girl. I swore I would never go to a hospital again, not even to give birth to children in one if it was up to me.

Life often unfolds in unexpected ways. During my first pregnancy, complications with my daughter required frequent ultrasounds and non-stress tests at the local hospital's birthing unit. My husband and I had originally planned for a birth at a small, homelike birthing center—but that option quickly slipped away.

To my surprise, the hospital experience was not what I had feared. The nurses treated me with kindness and respect, allowing me to make my own choices and honoring my voice in the process. For the first time, I felt truly seen—valued as an individual whose opinions mattered.

By the time my daughter was born—healthy, though affected by some prenatal nutritional deficits—my perspective had shifted dramatically. A year later, with her on my hip, I began my journey toward a nursing degree. That decision would lead to a fulfilling career that spanned more than three decades.

I see God's hand in all of it as He has guided me through so much joy, pain, and deep loss to help me become what I am today. I still struggle with much of what I see passed as "health care" today. I love to focus on prevention and healing rather than medical interventions, although those are necessary at times as well. Life is so much more than just asking the doctors, or taking the latest medication. We all have to take responsibility for our own wellness. I believe that passivity kills people.

As a believer in Jesus Christ and His redemptive work, I can confidently say that the greatest healing comes from receiving Him into your life. I have personally experienced His power—restoring both my soul and body. Choosing to trust in Christ is the most life-changing decision anyone can make. Don't wait. Embrace Him today. You'll never regret it, and the blessings will ripple through your life and into eternity—for you and those you love.

Perhaps you want to pray this simple prayer:

"Lord Jesus, I know I am a sinner. I know you came into this world to die for my sins so that I can have eternal life with you. Thank you that you have done the work, and all I have to do is accept your forgiveness. Thank you for being my good, good heavenly Father. I want to be your child forever. Amen."

If you did that, you are now born again into God's kingdom, just as Jesus described it in John 3. May the Lord be with you as you make your own journey of discovery into His immeasurable riches.

www.ingramcontent.com/pod-product-compliance
Lightning Source LLC
Chambersburg PA
CBHW071101120626
46546CB00003B/1242